WHAT YOUR COLLEAGUES ARE SAYING . . .

"I love this text. I think this text helps make coaching practicable."

Angela Becton
Consultant, Advanced Learning Consultant
Kinston, NC

"It is a very interesting book that is very needed during this time. It provides a clear path for effective coaching."

Tanna H. Nicely
Executive Principal, Knox County Schools
Blaine, TN

"I really liked this book and believe it would be a good tool for administrators who want to grow together or district teams to study how to improve their instructional coaching approach. This book is a good resource for administrators who want to improve their coaching techniques."

Courtney Miller
Founder, Inclusive Teachers Academy
Covina, CA

"Matt Renwick is the principal we all wish we had and the one we all want to be. His ideas about walking alongside teachers to grow them in the same ways we want them to grow students are just-right advice. He brings the research on trust and collective efficacy to life through concrete ways to operationalize rituals and routines of observation, goal setting, and planning with teachers."

Samantha Bennett
Learning Design Specialist, Instructional Coach, and
Education Consultant

"Matt Renwick makes a compelling case for deeper inquiry and more thoughtful engagement around teacher practice. Full of rich, compelling examples from Matt's real-world experience, this book will help readers reconnect with their purpose as instructional leaders. Highly recommended."

Justin Baeder
Director of The Principal Center and
Author of *Now We're Talking!*

"Matt Renwick offers readers a rich, practical how-to book supported by current research. This book should be within easy arm's reach of school administrators wishing to increase their skills of performing their major responsibility: increasing student learning."

Arthur L. Costa and Robert J. Garmston
Professors Emeriti, California State University, Sacramento, and
Co-Authors of *Cognitive Coaching*

"Matt Renwick reminds us of a key element of our shared professional leadership work: we can't do it alone. He keeps us focused on the value of coaching tools and the pillars he references to keep instruction at the center of the work of educational leaders. This book draws on an extensive research base as well as Matt Renwick's own professional experience to provide an accessible entry point for school leaders as they consider what it means to lead like a coach."

Jason Drysdale
Assistant Superintendent, River East Transcona
Winnipeg, Manitoba, Canada

"Research is clear: Principals can have a tremendous impact on student success by focusing on job #1: ensuring every student benefits from great teaching in every classroom. Drawing upon his vast experience as a successful leader, Matt Renwick provides compelling insights, practical tools, and real-life examples for how to effect real change in schools. *Leading Like a C.O.A.C.H.* is a must-read playbook for any principal seeking to improve student outcomes—not by forcing change from outside in, but rather by unleashing it from the inside out through trust, compassion, optimism, and an unrelenting focus on excellence."

Bryan Goodwin
President & CEO, McREL International, and
Author of *Building a Curious School*

"Renwick unpacks conversations by describing what he said in a coaching situation and then sharing his reasoning for why he chose the actions he took. This book is not just for people who are in the positional role of leader; it is for anyone who wants to develop their leadership capabilities."

Bena Kallick
Co-Director, Institute for Habits of Mind, and
Co-Author of *Students at the Center*)

"This is exactly the book educators need to build trust while navigating the tensions in today's school systems. *Leading Like a C.O.A.C.H.* will provide you with strategies that humanize leadership and bring joy to the work. This is an excellent book to read with your school teams to build the leadership pipeline essential to sustaining organizational excellence and a positive culture."

Anthony Kim
Founder and CEO, Education Elements, and
Co-Author of *The NEW School Rules*

"An inspirational guide for school leaders, this text provokes discussion and reflection among leaders who see themselves *as* co-leaders in school communities. School vision becomes a reality when school leaders coach school faculties in a collaborative and collegial way in order to create a comprehensive and cohesive learning environment for students. An excellent book that is accessible to all principals."

Allyson Matczuk
Early Literacy Consultant and Reading Recovery Trainer at Manitoba
Education and Training

"*Leading Like a C.O.A.C.H.* provides a framework that engenders trust and fortifies commitment to instructional excellence. Matt Renwick helps readers envision and rethink roles and routines. Most of all, his strategies, stories, and practical approach take the burden of trying to be an 'expert of everything' off of principals' shoulders. If you want your school to be a place where teachers and students want to be, this book is for you!"

Cris Tovani
English teacher, literacy consultant, and Author of
Why Do I Have to Read This?

LEADING LIKE A C.O.A.C.H.

Leading Like a C.O.A.C.H.

5 Strategies for Supporting Teaching and Learning

Matt Renwick

Foreword by Regie Routman

CORWIN

FOR INFORMATION:

Corwin

A SAGE Company

2455 Teller Road

Thousand Oaks, California 91320

(800) 233-9936

www.corwin.com

SAGE Publications Ltd.

1 Oliver's Yard

55 City Road

London EC1Y 1SP

United Kingdom

SAGE Publications India Pvt. Ltd.

B 1/I 1 Mohan Cooperative Industrial Area

Mathura Road, New Delhi 110 044

India

SAGE Publications Asia-Pacific Pte. Ltd.

18 Cross Street #10-10/11/12

China Square Central

Singapore 048423

President: Mike Soules

Associate Vice President
and Editorial Director: Monica Eckman

Senior Acquisitions
Editors: Ariel Curry and Tanya Ghans

Content Development
Manager: Desirée A. Bartlett

Senior Editorial
Assistant: Caroline Timmings

Editorial Assistant: Nancy Chung

Production Editor: Tori Mirsadjadi

Copy Editor: QuADS Prepress Pvt. Ltd.

Typesetter: C&M Digitals (P) Ltd.

Cover Designer: Gail Buschman

Marketing Manager: Morgan Fox

Printed in Canada

Library of Congress Cataloging-in-Publication Data

Names: Renwick, Matt, author.

Title: Leading like a C.O.A.C.H. : 5 strategies for supporting teaching and learning / Matt Renwick.

Other titles: Leading like a coach

Description: Thousand Oaks, California : Corwin, 2022. | Includes bibliographical references and index.

Identifiers: LCCN 2021045749 | ISBN 9781071840474 (paperback) | ISBN 9781071840467 (epub) | ISBN 9781071840450 (epub) | ISBN 9781071840443 (pdf)

Subjects: LCSH: Educational leadership. | Educators—Professional relationships. | School management and organization.

Classification: LCC LB2806 .R384 2022 | DDC 371.2/011—dc23/eng/20211013

LC record available at https://lccn.loc.gov/2021045749

This book is printed on acid-free paper.

22 23 24 25 26 10 9 8 7 6 5 4 3 2 1

CONTENTS

FOREWORD

In his groundbreaking book, *Leading Like a C.O.A.C.H.,* principal Matt Renwick re-envisions the roles of the principal as supportive guide, active listener, learner-teacher, and opportunity creator. With humility and deep knowledge, Matt provides the conditions, actions, demonstrations, and language that make it possible to create a trusting, collaborative, and responsive school culture. We accompany the author on his learning journey, get inside his thinking/changing/reflecting process, and come to rethink and expand our own thinking, expectations, and possibilities about literacy and leadership.

While coaching well is central to effective leadership, it is embracing a coaching stance in service to empowering teachers and learners that is at the heart of this book. School leaders are invited to rethink the primary role and identity of the principal as learning partner, not chief evaluator. It is the principal taking a nonjudgmental, compassionate view of coaching—noticing and appreciating what's going well in the classroom and school *before* focusing on needs. It's about seeing and commenting on teachers' strengths and efforts, about treating them, their students, and their families with respect and compassion. It's about giving agency and authority to teachers, learning from them, and creating opportunities for both teachers and students to take the lead and ably chart their own leadership and learning path.

The author states the main benefits of leading like a coach:

- Building trust and positive relationships with faculty members
- Having a more positive impact on teaching and learning
- Improving the quality of feedback to and from teachers
- Developing collaborative independence among the staff

Over the decade I've known Matt, as both an esteemed colleague and a friend, I've been impressed with his openness to new ways of thinking and willingness to reconsider his beliefs and practices—even when initially skeptical. He is a scholar and deep thinker. He pays attention to research. He listens to other educators. Like all highly effective leaders and teachers, he is always questioning, reflecting, and learning. He demonstrates the power of literacy "as the common thread of all disciplines. Where schools make a conscious effort to develop better readers and writers, every subject area improves."

Because I have come to know Matt well, I can assert that the changes he has made as a leader are profound and lasting. He came to learn that giving teachers and students opportunities to share their thinking *is* instructional time. He questioned and rethought some of his prior beliefs and practices. He let go of controlling each situation so that the power structure between principal and teachers—and teachers and students—became more equitable. He came to observe teachers with an open heart and mind and to learn from them. He states, "It was I who initially needed the coaching."

It was through daily instructional walks that Matt began to question his prior assumptions about teaching and learning. Because these visits are affirming and supportive to teachers, they come to welcome these frequent visits, to treasure the immediate recognition they receive from their principal, and to be more open to constructive feedback. The coaching conversations that are integral to instructional walks are akin to a delicate dance, artfully choreographed where the person who takes the lead (initially the principal) is supportive and non-threatening—gently nudging, encouraging, demonstrating, and guiding so the partner (the teacher) is able to assume a more leading role. Throughout the entire book, there are many examples of coaching conversations, which include the actual language used by the principal and the teacher. Coaching conversations, which are at the heart of expert teaching and leading, can also serve as models for teacher conversations with peers and students.

What each chapter has in common is how to explicitly engage in the work of leading like a coach; guide teachers to think critically about their practices; use demonstrations and coaching conversations to help build teachers' confidence, trust, and openness to suggestions; and promote self-directed teaching and learning for themselves and their students.

As a reader-leader, we explicitly learn how, when, and why to

- develop and sustain schoolwide trust as foundational to effective leadership and learning;

- give more agency and authority to teachers—and students;

- communicate feedback effectively—through paraphrasing, pausing, and posing questions;

- create more leadership opportunities for teachers;

- engage in ongoing, professional learning focused on foundations of literacy;

- establish shared beliefs, norms, and goals and apply promising literacy practices;

- create opportunities for schoolwide improvement across the curriculum;

- establish excellent, accessible-to-all classroom libraries with and by students;

- see obstacles as opportunities; and

- reflect on the results of our actions and behaviors.

Ultimately, the main purpose of instructional walks and each of the instructional frameworks detailed in *Leading Like a C.O.A.C.H* is to enhance teaching and learning effectiveness and enjoyment; build an equitable, schoolwide culture of high achievement, trust, and ongoing collaboration; and foster leadership beyond the principal. Matt reminds us, "The goal of *Leading Like a C.O.A.C.H* is nurturing self-directed leaders and learners among your staff: developing a school culture that can sustain itself beyond one's tenure." With that important goal in mind, Matt continues to lead by example: highlighting strengths of his capable staff, listening more and advising less, and seeking to ensure teachers drive the important conversations about teaching and learning. In *Leading Like a C.O.A.C.H*, Matt has gifted us with frameworks of possibilities for transformational leadership.

—Regie Routman, October 2021

ACKNOWLEDGMENTS

I would like to say thanks to the following people:

To Jodi, Finn, and Violet for their patience and their unconditional love.

To my parents and the rest of my family for their encouragement and support of my work.

To the Mineral Point Unified School District teachers, staff, students, and families for allowing me to document and celebrate all the positive aspects of our learning community.

To Regie Routman for her collegiality, her friendship, and her generosity with her time and talents.

To the CESA 3 team and all the area school leaders for partnering with me in this professional learning.

To Jamie Ciconetti and Rita Platt for their initial feedback on the manuscript.

To Kelly Jones and Ron Lott for providing feedback for the book along with their guidance in all things on instructional coaching.

To Mary Beth Nicklaus, Matt Cormier, Jason Drysdale, Arlis Folkerts, Allyson Matczuk, and Mario Beauchamp for their willingness to share their professional stories with me.

To Ariel Curry, Desirée Bartlett, and the rest of the Corwin team for their smart insights and their consistent encouragement to make this book the best it can be.

PUBLISHER'S ACKNOWLEDGMENTS

Corwin gratefully acknowledges the contributions of the following reviewers:

Angela Becton
Advanced Learning Consultant
Kinston, NC

Ronda Gray
Clinical Associate Professor
Department of Teacher Education
University of Illinois at Springfield
Decatur, IL

Chanel Johnson
Science Specialist
Atlanta, GA

Courtney Miller
Founder of the Inclusive Teachers Academy
Covina, CA

Saundra Mouton
Instructional Coach
Briarmeadow Charter School
Katy, TX

Tanna H. Nicely
Executive Principal
Knox County Schools
Blaine, TN

Jay Posick
Principal
Merton Intermediate School
Hartland, WI

Kathy Rhodes
Principal
Hinton Community School
Hinton, IA

Jim Thompson
Video Instructional Coach
Penfield, NY

ABOUT THE AUTHOR

Matt Renwick is an elementary school principal in Mineral Point, Wisconsin. Previously he served as an assistant principal, athletic director, coach, and classroom teacher in Wisconsin Rapids, Wisconsin. He was recognized as a Friend of Literacy by the Wisconsin State Reading Association in 2020 and received the Kohl Leadership Award in 2021. His other works include *5 Myths About Classroom Technology: How do we integrate digital tools to truly enhance learning?* (2016) and *Digital Portfolios in the Classroom: Showcasing and Assessing Student Work* (2017). You can find Matt on Twitter @ReadbyExample and at mattrenwick.com.

INTRODUCTION

This is not a traditional "school leadership" book. Rather, I offer an integrated and more mindful approach to educational improvement. Anyone in a leadership position—coaches, department heads, principals, specialists, district administrators—can adopt the ideas offered here to help a school more fully realize its potential.

This book is written from the belief that, just as every student has the potential to grow and succeed, all schools have the capacity for instructional excellence. And schools that have leaders who adopt a coaching stance as part of their practice are more likely to realize this success. This success is not only for the students and the faculty. You will also become more effective in guiding a learning organization toward positive change.

Leaders achieve success *with* their teachers, their students, and their families. If we see ourselves as part of a larger system, and not solely responsible for the outcomes, then we can become co-authors who collectively write our own school's story.

Education and other systems have become more complex over time. In response, outside organizations have tried to simplify our work with crude assessments (i.e., standardized testing) and overly complicated evaluation processes. Their good intentions have often disrupted the positive narratives we are trying to craft.

With that, it is unrealistic for any leader to strive to achieve school-wide excellence alone. Principals, specialists, department heads, and district-level administrators cannot be in every classroom at every moment. Therefore, teachers must become more self-monitoring and self-directed. This occurs when leaders recognize what is already going well while conveying confidence that teachers have the capacity for reflection and renewal. These are the conditions for professional growth.

Leading like a coach fosters instructional improvement by first acknowledging all the excellent practices currently present. We create the environment for change by noting where we are already successful. These practices build trust, which then allows for more constructive feedback. Over time a sense of community, that we can only do this together, becomes the norm for the culture of a school.

THE PURPOSE OF THIS BOOK

This resource is an authentic and adaptive response to this complexity. There are too many moving parts within education to effectively attend to them all. To manage and lead today means focusing on a few key aspects of instructional leadership. With more than 20 years of experience as a teacher and administrator, as well as discovering what research and other leaders have found effective, I have learned there are four primary areas of focus that lead to schoolwide success:

➤ **C**reate Confidence through Trust

➤ **O**rganize Around a Priority

➤ **A**ffirm Promising Practices

➤ **C**ommunicate Feedback

These tenets align with the vision for any leader:

➤ **H**elp Teachers Become Leaders and Learners

Helping teachers become leaders and learners ensures that a school becomes more self-directed and sustainable over time (Costa et al., 2016; Routman, 2014). Together they form the acronym "C.O.A.C.H." (Figure I.1). It is a framework that leaders can operate within as they visit classrooms and interact with students and staff.

While this book organizes these principles as chapters in a linear fashion, you can take up any area at any time. One is not necessarily dependent on the other. Think of it as a mosaic. The unifying

Figure I.1   C.O.A.C.H. framework as a mosaic

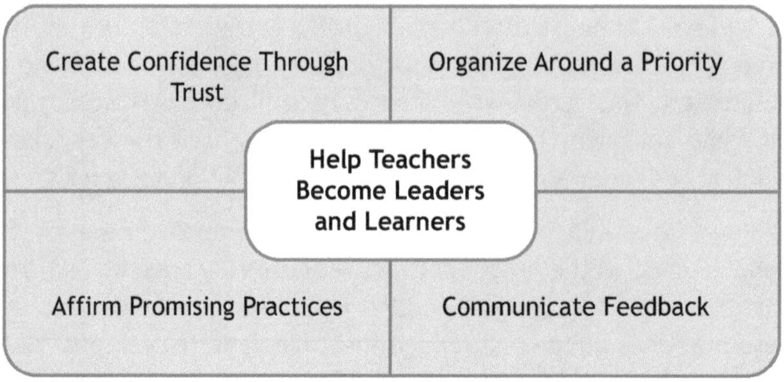

Create Confidence Through Trust	Organize Around a Priority
Help Teachers Become Leaders and Learners	
Affirm Promising Practices	Communicate Feedback

theme here is each principle asks that we embrace the identity as a coach, one who supports and improves teachers' thinking processes and resources to achieve goals while enhancing self-directed learning (Costa et al., 2016). The vehicle for engaging in coaching practices are *instructional walks*, informal classroom visits in which leaders "are looking first for the teachers' strengths, noticing where support is needed, and also discerning instructional patterns across a school" (Routman, 2014, p. 198).

Maybe the most important thing to know about instructional walks is they are a process, not a singular event. They serve to inform both teachers and leaders about instruction over time, with the goal of developing faculty members' capacity for self-directed learning and professional renewal.

Next are the steps for one walk within this process.

THE INSTRUCTIONAL WALK PROCESS

- Step 1: Share Your Intentions With Your Staff
  - Discuss the instructional walk plan and rationale with teacher leaders.
  - Introduce instructional walks at a staff meeting.
  - Follow up with an email before beginning walks.
  - Describe and clarify how walks are connected to the school priority.
- Step 2: Start Visiting Classrooms
  - Schedule visits at random times and come in unannounced.
  - Take a stance of curiosity and seeking to learn (vs. judging).
  - Write down what you observe: dialogue, actions, environment.
  - Briefly summarize what occurred and how students benefited.
- Step 3: Engaging in Conversations
  - Hand notes to the teacher after scanning them into a digital application.
  - Affirm publicly what went well—three to five aspects of instruction.
  - When appropriate, ask questions about the teacher's decision-making.
  - Follow up on these discussion points during future instructional walks.

I have found many benefits when instructional walks are utilized daily:

▶ *Trust increases:* Teachers see my positive intentions and start to associate my presence in their classrooms as supportive and constructive.

▶ *Stress decreases:* When more of my visits are focused on learning versus judging, teachers become more relaxed when a formal observation occurs.

▶ *Feedback is welcomed:* As I regularly highlight what is going well, opportunities are found for more constructive feedback and reflection around a teacher's practice.

▶ *Teachers become coaches for each other:* Making my approach and process visible serves as a model for faculty members to collaborate with their colleagues.

▶ *Authority is shifted to classrooms:* By giving agency to faculty, the responsibility for positive learning outcomes is released to teachers and students.

The ideas suggested in this book to realize these benefits come from a principal's perspective. Yet any school leader—including teacher leaders—can apply these ideas to their practice.

This may not be the only journey toward success, yet it is one I am confident any leader can follow and personalize to their own situation. So where do we begin? It helps to remember why we became educators in the first place and the pathway we walked to the present day.

MY COACHING JOURNEY

My interest in education came out of a desire to make a positive impact on the lives of students. My first step on my journey was coaching my hometown's Little League and girls' softball teams right out of high school. My experience and interest in baseball served me well. What also helped was the straightforward nature of the sport. Throw strikes. Wait for your pitch. Get a healthy lead. I could teach my players these skills within the context of the game and, subsequently, we saw consistent results.

As a teacher, I learned that classroom instruction was not the same as coaching sports. For instance, there was not always a clear instructional goal. We had to establish our own measures of success. As an example, we designed projects, such as building toothpick bridges during math to test the strength of different geometrical shapes. My students and I also engaged in service learning, such as testing for pollutants in a local creek and publishing the results to show understanding.

I also discovered that, if true learning were to take place, my students had to be committed to these goals. They needed to feel empowered in helping determine how the classroom operated, including what books to read, what topics to write about, and how their understanding would be represented with more authentic assessments. This understanding, of co-creating the conditions and environment, came from my graduate studies that included resources like *Improving Schools From Within* by Roland Barth (1990). It carried over into my leadership career.

My learning continued. As a secondary assistant principal and an elementary principal, I discovered the following:

- True change comes from within, and my role as a leader is to not change people but to support them in their own process of continuous self-renewal (*Cognitive Coaching*, Costa et al., 2016).

- I can best support my faculty by first noticing their strengths, recognizing their efforts, and celebrating their successes along their professional learning journeys (*Read, Write, Lead*, Routman, 2014).

- Through trusting others and being trustworthy, I create confidence within others and myself to start considering opportunities for improvement (*Trust Matters*, Tschannen-Moran, 2014).

- By organizing my school's resources, strategies, and time around what we deem is a priority, I can be more focused and present during classroom visits (*The NEW School Rules*, Kim & Gonzalez-Black, 2018).

- Classroom visits that first affirm teachers' successes can lead to better conversations with teachers around their practice (*Now We're Talking!*, Baeder, 2018).

- Feedback is most effective when I directly engage with my teachers (*Reducing Change to Increase Improvement*, Robinson, 2018) and differentiate how I communicate based on their way of knowing (*Tell Me So I Can Hear You*, Drago-Severson & Blum-DeStefano, 2016).

My learning is continuous. And while the literature and research in the field are important, they are best supported when interacting with the individuals positioned to realize our collective goal: teachers guiding students to become self-directed and continuous learners themselves.

SPECIAL NOTE: THIS IS NOT A "COACHING" BOOK

While the principles described here are aligned with effective coaching practices, such as some of the strategies described by Knight (2010) and Sweeney (2010), this is not a "coaching" book. We instead look to adopt some elements and skills of coaching within our roles, including teacher goal setting, co-creating a plan for learning, collecting data, and analyzing the results for improvement.

Recent studies support leading like a coach. For example, a 2021 meta-analysis about what effective principals do found that one of the primary traits of effective principals was "engaging in instructionally focused interactions with teachers" (Grissom et al., 2021). These "forms of engagement with teachers" include experiences that "center on instructional practice, such as teacher evaluation, *instructional coaching*, and the establishment of a data-driven, schoolwide instructional program to facilitate such interactions" (Grissom et al., 2021, p. xv, my emphasis). Worth noting: "Engaging in instructionally focused interactions with teachers" is the first finding listed in the report.

Coaching is focused interaction. It is, at its core, a conversation among colleagues about teaching and learning. These conversations are founded on trust, aligned with a priority, and supported with evidence collected from classroom visits (instructional walks) that are both positive and constructive in their approach.

 # Reflective Questions

I now invite you to reflect on your own learning journey toward becoming a leader.

[*Within each chapter you will find reflection activities. You may want to devote a notebook to these written activities so that you can keep all of your thoughts together in one place to reference at a later time.*]

- Why did you get into education?

- What did you first believe about teaching and learning? Why?

- How did you come to change your beliefs?

- What books, resources, and thought leaders have informed your thinking and your professional learning journey to today?

- What next step might you take on this journey? Why?

In addition to reflective questions at the end of each chapter, expect the following features:

- *Examples:* Narratives showing how these ideas have been implemented in classrooms and schools

- *Activities:* Invitations to apply the strategies and skills described in the Examples

- *Special Notes:* Address a topic or question that relates to the chapter's focus

- *Success Indicators:* What to expect over time as you adopt these practices

- *Wisdom From the Field:* Stories that exemplify what it means to lead more like a coach

CONCLUSION: A BETTER VERSION OF OURSELVES

Just as there should be more to sports than only wins and losses, leading like a coach in schools is about more than assessment results and state rankings. It is about helping everyone to become a better version of themselves.

Leaders are included in this journey. As you visit classrooms regularly with purpose and curiosity, you will start to feel more confident in your knowledge about the subject matter and instruction in your school. You will see patterns, both positive and negative, and then consider constructive next steps that honor teachers' professionalism and address students' needs. This learning is job-embedded, which makes it even more powerful because students can directly benefit.

This book will serve as your guide to engage directly with teaching and learning in classrooms. Following these principles, the educational experience will no longer be measured solely by test scores and evaluation systems. The narrative you have created together will be more accurate than any outsider could attempt to define. And you believe in this narrative because you are creating your own story within it: from someone who struggles to see their impact on student learning, to a true leader who sees their influence making a real difference in their school community.

Let's begin!

WHY SHOULD I LEAD LIKE A COACH?

Identity is the mental model each of us constructs of who we are as a unique self. This is an important concept because identity informs decisions and behaviors. The most sustainable way to change behaviors is to change identity.

—Costa et al. (2016, p. 25)

In my first year as a principal in Mineral Point, Wisconsin, I made it a point to be visible in classrooms by scheduling daily visits. The main purpose was to be present.

In one fourth-grade classroom, students were writing independently or conferring with the teacher or a classmate to get feedback about their draft so far. I stopped by one student, his eyes gazing forward, seemingly lost in thought. Assuming he was considering what to write next, I asked, "What are you writing about?" He explained his topic. Then I asked, "And who are you writing for?"

The classroom teacher was close by and overheard my questions. It resonated with her, as she brought it up later during a conversation. "You know, your questions reminded me that kids need an audience for their writing. I realized they did not have one for that task."

I was not sure what to say. My intention had not been to critique. I was simply going off my own philosophy—that a writer should have both a purpose and an audience. I responded with a humble "Well, I am glad I was helpful," and went on my way.

Any positive impact on teaching and learning need not be accidental. Nor should we only be present in classrooms for the sake of accountability. Let's instead lead with intention and with the confidence that we can make a positive difference. If we believe in our potential and know it to be true, we start to live it out as if it is our current reality.

> If we believe in our potential and know it to be true, we start to live it out as if it is our current reality.

Leaders can develop this self-confidence by adopting as default a curious, purposeful, and supportive stance when observing instruction. So where to begin? Before we can take our first step forward, we need to reimagine our position beyond "administrator," "dean," "principal," or "specialist" in our schools and embrace the idea of *leading like a coach*. This chapter begins this journey for leaders: describing the specific benefits and how to embrace a coaching stance as a primary identity.

BENEFITS OF LEADING LIKE A COACH

> Leading like a coach is not just a preferred approach; it can be the primary way we conduct ourselves, an identity we adopt in all classrooms to support everyone's journey toward renewal.

One of our most important roles as leaders is hiring great teachers. Yet if that were all it took to lead excellent schools, our educational challenges would be resolved. Thankfully, we are in positions to better support instructional improvement if we can rethink our roles.

Continuous improvement is the default position in successful organizations. There are conditions that once in place can cultivate this healthy growth, including trust, focus, and curiosity. "Best practices" and other dualistic ways of seeing our work become outdated. Leadership starts to be perceived as a concept that anyone can adopt versus a position.

Therefore, leading like a coach is not just a preferred approach; it can be the primary way we conduct ourselves, an identity we adopt in all classrooms to support everyone's journey toward renewal. Consider the next four reasons for expanding our role in this way.

BENEFITS OF LEADING LIKE A COACH

1. You will build trust and positive relationships with faculty members.

2. You will have a more positive impact on teaching and learning.

3. You will improve the quality of feedback between yourself and your teachers.

4. You will help develop collaborative independence among your staff.

YOU WILL BUILD TRUST AND POSITIVE RELATIONSHIPS WITH FACULTY MEMBERS

Trust and relationships are a prerequisite for schoolwide improvement. Taking a coaching stance as a leader can foster trust and build relationships while engaging in instructional improvement.

Dr. Jenny Edwards, who wrote a chapter in Costa et al.'s (2016) *Cognitive Coaching*, found that teachers who were supervised by administrators trained in instructional coaching reported feeling more supported than from leaders' classroom walkthroughs. These teachers indicated that, because of their administrators' coaching stance, they were better able to reflect on their practice and gain insights. Their trust in administration also increased, evident by their improved willingness to share ideas with building principals (Costa et al., 2016, p. 279).

When we take a less evaluative stance with many of our classroom visits and are clear about our intentions, teachers can relax more. They know what to expect. Expectations for success lead to a cycle of effective performance, important for *Creating Confidence Through Trust* (a topic we examine more closely in Chapter 3).

YOU WILL HAVE A MORE POSITIVE IMPACT ON TEACHING AND LEARNING

A prevailing myth is that an administrator or formal leader cannot engage in coaching conversations or lead any type of instructional coaching in general. This is rationalized by those who believe that if someone is your supervisor, they also cannot coach you.

Studies have shown this to be inaccurate. Again, research curated by Dr. Jenny Edwards describes the positive impact a leader can have when taking a coaching stance, for teachers and for a leader's own practice (Costa et al., 2016):

- Administrators who were trained as coaches were asked to reflect on an experience in which they used their coaching skills as part of their positions. They believed they were able to apply these coaching skills successfully. Participating administrators also found they grew in their own practice and in their appreciation of instructional coaching in general (p. 252).

- In a study examining the effects of teachers coached by an administrator, by another teacher, or by a specialist, the results indicated that *there was no difference in who the teacher was coached by*—professional growth was a result regardless (p. 255; my emphasis).

To be clear, having an instructional coach in one's school is preferred. They can often engage in more confidential conversations with faculty members about their practice. Regardless of roles, what is critical for professional growth to occur is clarity and specificity around common beliefs and practices for classrooms. This is discussed more in Chapter 4, *Organize Around a Priority*.

WISDOM FROM THE FIELD: ALL LEADERS CAN BE COACHES

Education is not the only profession where leading like a coach is recommended. In an article for *Harvard Business Review*, Ibarra and Scoular (2019) argue that a direct approach to business leadership is no longer effective in a highly complex world. "Rapid, constant, and disruptive change is now the norm, and what succeeded in the past is no longer a guide to what will succeed in the future. Twenty-first century managers simply don't (and can't!) have all the right answers." They recommend leaders "give support and guidance rather than instructions" to be a more effective entrepreneur and supervisor.

Knowing that leadership in multiple professions is going through similar changes, does this information help validate your interest in leading more like a coach? Jot down your ideas and thoughts in your journal.

YOU WILL IMPROVE THE QUALITY OF FEEDBACK BETWEEN YOURSELF AND YOUR TEACHERS

In working with other school leaders shifting toward a coaching stance, one of the primary reasons they cite for not visiting classrooms regularly is being unsure about what they should be doing or how they might engage with teachers about their practice. They are concerned about saying too much and offending someone, or they lack confidence about what to say at all. Subsequently, regular classroom visits often consist of either formal observations where stakes are high, or simple check-ins to say "Good morning" to the students and staff.

What teachers crave and leaders want is to facilitate feedback that moves instruction forward. In fact, "people need feedback so desperately that, in the absence of actual feedback, they will invent it" (Costa et al., 2016, p. 53). Yet the opportunity for professional learning can be inhibited by formal observations.

For example, Grissom and Loeb (2017) found that due to the high stakes of teacher evaluations, school leaders tend to give teachers higher evaluation ratings than they would necessarily merit. This is potentially due to teacher evaluation results being associated with recommendations for renewal or nonrenewal. Conversely, the researchers found leaders were more honest about a teacher's performance when the situation was low stakes. This study supports the development of a coaching context—by being clear about our intentions when adopting a formative stance to create a safe space for professional learning.

When the stakes are low and leaders become more curious instead of critical about instruction, professional learning flourishes. Khachatryan (2015) analyzed feedback delivered from a principal to multiple teachers in one school. Her findings revealed that feedback that focused more on process was correlated with an increase in teachers' desire for professional growth. Conversely, more judgmental feedback (a common element of formal observations) was correlated with teachers becoming ambivalent or even resistant to these interactions.

In other words, when a leader both *affirms promising practices* and *effectively communicates feedback* about how to continue to grow (later addressed in Chapters 5 and 6), teaching improves. These practices are at the heart of leading like a coach and are embedded within the instructional walk process.

SPECIAL NOTE: WHY ALL THE LITERACY EXAMPLES?

This book will provide several real-life examples from classrooms that illustrate what leading like a coach looks like. Most examples take place within a literacy context. What about mathematics, science, social studies, or other important disciplines? Here are a few reasons.

- *My school's priority has been literacy:* Developing readers, writers, communicators, and thinkers has been the focus in the schools I have had the privilege of leading. Our assessment results have supported this direction. This information is to simply acknowledge the limits in the examples you will read here.

- *Your school's priority should probably be literacy, too:* I avoided stating "should" throughout this text, except here. However you look at it, literacy is in need of improvement in our schools. As one piece of evidence, the 2019 National Assessment of Educational Progress scores revealed that the majority of states had lower achievement results in eighth-grade reading when compared with 2017 (U.S. Department of Education, 2019).

- *Literacy is the common thread of all disciplines:* When schools make a conscious effort to develop better readers and writers, every subject area benefits. Likewise, students' literacy skills improve when authentically integrated with other disciplines. The content is typically high-interest and provides background knowledge for students to better engage in their learning.

If you believe literacy should not be a focus of your school improvement work because you have achieved sustainable success, congratulations! I would love to profile your journey toward excellence; contact me at mattrenwick.com or on Twitter at @ReadByExample. Thankfully, leading like a coach is not exclusive to one discipline because it is about *improving instructional practices*. You are encouraged to explore other areas for improvement. The strategies described here are applicable to any priority.

YOU WILL HELP DEVELOP COLLABORATIVE INDEPENDENCE AMONG YOUR STAFF

The word *coach* comes from the Hungarian concept of a horse-drawn coach that takes a person from one place to another (Costa et al., 2016, p. 19). The person being coached, the client, has their "hands on the reins" and is driving the agenda for the work.

When we adopt a coaching stance in our interactions with teachers, we are in service to a larger purpose instead of an outside or personal agenda. This process of examining one's own practice with a partner, such as collecting and analyzing student learning results to understand the impact of instruction and make changes, can be our default stance.

Yet improvement in isolation does not lead to collective excellence. We need networks and structures for mutual support, so all educators have access to effective approaches. This can be described as "both independent and interdependent" (Costa et al., 2016) or "collaborative independence" (Johnston et al., 2020). Collaborative independence means directing one's own teaching and learning within a broader community of professionals that cultivates a safe environment for innovation and risk-taking.

Leading like a coach can foster collaborative independence among faculty. Because of the reciprocal nature of coaching, in which the coach learns as much as the person being coached, knowledge tends to spread more rapidly. For example, a leader may share what they learned in one classroom with another teacher. They can talk about someone else's practice with a sense of reverence and admiration, instead of trying to offer advice about best practice. The possibility of professional collaboration increases as effective teaching practices start to permeate throughout the school.

The possibility of professional collaboration increases as effective teaching practices start to permeate throughout the school.

Developing collaborative independence ultimately enhances the culture, where professional inquiry and growth become acceptable and eventually even expected. Questions about practice become an indicator of strength instead of a sign of weakness. Teachers become the leaders that they were meant to be and the learners they already are.

EXPAND ON YOUR CURRENT IDENTITIES

If you listed all your duties and roles as a leader, it would be quite long. Supervisor, counselor, student advocate, and parent resource come to my mind right away. When you go home, you likely have multiple roles there as well—for example, parent, caretaker, spouse, relative, neighbor, or friend. Our multiple identities describe unique roles within the different worlds we inhabit.

Related, we readily shift between one identity and another. For example, when I leave my office after a post-observation conference with a teacher to help monitor lunch, I am flexible in my capacity to serve the needs of different situations.

So to adopt the stance of a coach as part of our larger identity as leader is attainable. Likely some faculty members in your school have already accomplished this. For example, instructional coaches and staff developers take on multiple identities while working with teachers. Lipton and Wellman (2007) make this distinction in describing three stances instructional coaches take:

1. Coaching (teacher is the primary source of information and analysis)

2. Collaborating (specialist and teacher co-develop ideas and co-analyze situations, work products, and other data, once they have clarified the problem)

3. Consulting (specialist supplies information, identifies and analyzes gaps, suggests solutions, thinks aloud about cause-and-effect relationships, and makes connections to principles of practice)

So too can school leaders move beyond the notion that their role begins and ends with managing school operations and leading instructional improvement from a distance. We can expand our leadership role and adopt a coaching stance as the situation warrants.

ACTIVITY 1.1 — EXPAND ON YOUR CURRENT IDENTITIES

To practice embracing multiple roles within one position, break down one area of your life by its different identities and list the duties and actions. The purpose is to examine (and appreciate) the complexity of our position as leaders, as well as to consider what is possible. Here is my example from my life at home:

Father

- Take care of my kids and keep them safe
- Ensure they are keeping up with school tasks
- Guide them to become independent

Husband

- Love and care for my wife
- Share the household duties
- Discuss family goals and how to achieve them, i.e., budget

Son and Sibling

- Check in with family members regularly
- Coordinate gatherings with parents, siblings, and relatives
- Acknowledge birthdays and special days/events

I admit that I do not meet each commitment with 100% success all the time. For example, I am notorious for not checking in over the phone. But I am aware of it, I believe I can improve in this area, and so I included this aspect of being a son and a sibling. Now I am actively working on it.

After reading this example, consider where you might begin to examine your own role as a school leader. How could you start to adopt an identity as a coach? Jot down some ideas in your journal. List at least three responsibilities a coach might fulfill.

SHIFTING TOWARD A COACHING STANCE

Our professional days feel full. Sometimes we barely have time to complete our annual observations as part of our educator evaluation systems, let alone get into classrooms for more informal visits. Time scarcity is a reality that deserves to be acknowledged.

One example: a principal I mentored was overseeing two schools. She had ample experience as a teacher prior to this position, which helped with immediate respect from the faculty. She had walked the walk in their eyes.

However, leading two buildings is challenging for anyone. During a tour of one of her schools, we found space in the library to chat. Setting our bags and coats down on a table, she announced, "Welcome to my office." While I appreciated being surrounded by books, I expressed surprise that she did not have a space dedicated to her work.

"How do you manage student discipline, or facilitate conversations that require privacy?" I asked. She pointed to a small office space nearby. "I am letting the reading interventionist use what was formally the principal's office; she didn't have anywhere to teach. I can use that space if needed." I felt reluctant to encourage her to start engaging in coaching conversations with so much on her plate and no place to call home.

The ideas and recommendations offered here are not designed to add to one's day, but rather to rethink what our days might become. Not to throw out what we currently have, but to revisit our current perspective and adjust the lenses, like a visit to the optometrist. The next comparisons describe these distinctions as we shift toward a coaching stance.

CO-DEVELOPING A VISION FOR SUCCESS (VS. FORMING A GOAL)

Leading like a coach involves co-creating goals, beliefs, and values that serve as steppingstones toward a larger vision. Any preferred outcomes, such as improved results from a traditional assessment, can also incorporate ways of knowing whether students saw themselves as successful. In addition, teachers and students would also be able to self-monitor their growth toward personalized goals within that vision.

The authors of *Cognitive Coaching* ask leaders to "develop a vision with your school staff and community—a vision that inspires the staff toward an important aim" (Costa et al., 2016, p. 311). This vision extends everyone's perspective beyond only proximal goals to "the future into which teachers, students, and parents gaze" and with the belief that "there is always more distance to travel" (Costa et al., 2016, p. 311).

As an example, I worked with teachers to develop a portfolio assessment process for English learners. It would be an alternative tool to the standardized exam students had to take yearly. We recognized that we were not only developing this process to determine if English learners were proficient and could graduate out of their support services. The larger purpose was to create a more culturally responsive system that better honored their language and background. Equity was the vision; a better assessment system was the goal.

This is not typical. Usually, only expected results are developed as part of an evaluation process (sometimes referred to as a "school learning objective," or SLO). Goals are important. But without context, inspiration, or a clear plan for success, they ring hollow.

For instance, in my first year as a head principal, we set a goal of a 10% increase in our students' writing scores from fall to spring. Yet we did not examine more deeply *why* we wanted to increase writing scores, or whether the results really meant our students had learned. For example, would more students see themselves as writers than before?

The goal was technical and lacked a vision for the broader purpose of our organization.

When we adopt a coaching stance, we maintain a focus on the larger purpose while also moving toward indicators of success. And if we are not satisfied with the results, then a faculty responds together to the current reality and notes it as part of our story toward success instead of blaming others or ourselves. In my experience, coaches who help a group envision what they genuinely want to achieve, on the field or in classrooms, have been able to foster greater purpose with their efforts that transcends only results.

Leading like a coach involves co-creating goals, beliefs, and values that serve as steppingstones toward a larger vision.

EMBRACING CHALLENGES AS OPPORTUNITIES (VS. IDENTIFYING AREAS FOR IMPROVEMENT)

When leading like a coach, we acknowledge any shortcomings within the *broader understanding of an organization's strengths, challenges, and possibilities.* Leaders as coaches start by celebrating what has been going well and why we believe that to be true, as well as what we have accomplished to reach a certain point. Every school has something to be proud of. By surfacing the stories and artifacts of our successes, we create a collective mindset that we as educators have a positive impact on our students. Obstacles become opportunities.

Yet leaders cannot simply reframe how people perceive situations. It also requires assessment and reflection. As Costa et al. (2016) note in *Cognitive Coaching*, "smart groups see encounters as learning opportunities. They use both formal and informal means of assessing what is working and what needs refinement. Reflection is the key to growth" (p. 314).

Schools determine a goal based on an area for improvement. For example, reading proficiency levels between students with and without disabilities may be a focus. This makes sense. The problem is not in improving in an area where we could grow, but that we too often approach it with a deficit mindset. When leaders state "Our students with special needs are not proficient readers," staff may hear "We are not effective reading teachers of students with special needs," or "Our students are not effective learners." People start to believe they are lacking or incapable. Again, we perpetuate the "schools need to be fixed" mindset when we position ourselves in this way.

Perceiving our challenges with an appreciative lens reinforces the vision and offers a positive pathway toward success. Any object of our

> By surfacing the stories and artifacts of our successes, we create a collective mindset that we as educators have a positive impact on our students. Obstacles become opportunities.

attention, such as assessment results, is the same regardless of how we view them. Why not view them as opportunities for growth?

ENGAGING IN PROFESSIONAL LEARNING (VS. DELIVERING PROFESSIONAL DEVELOPMENT)

By adopting a coaching stance, *we engage in professional learning*. A group of leaders, including teachers, can reach consensus on next steps for professional improvement.

This learning is not just for faculty. As a leader, I find that I learn as much as anyone when acting as a coach. It is impossible for me to know all the inner workings of instruction at each grade level and within each department—a primary reason I engage in instructional walks. By becoming curious about the teaching and learning happening in our classrooms, I can become more knowledgeable about the practices we currently employ while at the same time supporting implementation of new ideas.

One relevant learning experience for me was during a primary grade level's conversation around literacy skills. We were discussing decoding words, and someone added "encoding." I asked, "Encoding . . . you mean, writing and speaking?" I had not served at this level during my teaching career. They confirmed. Seeing myself as part of the learning experience versus delivering it helped keep my ego in check and stay open to new ideas. It also reminded me that time for collaboration and professional conversation is essential for our success.

As leaders with unique vantage points and our assigned responsibilities, we have some authority in how the school proceeds with staff development. Data trends and patterns can inform our decisions. Yet our positions alone do not ensure increased understanding. For example, have we broadened our perspective by gathering insights from the classroom experience, talking with teachers and students about their learning?

Professional learning plans are an opportunity for shared engagement. Reconsider whether it be "administered" to someone else, as if we are inoculating a school against future failure. It is disappointing to hear teachers share how infrequently their leaders visit during instruction. Leading from a distance is like teaching a science unit on water systems but never having the students touch water. We cannot fully understand anything unless we experience it firsthand and with the point of view of others involved.

EXAMINE POSSIBILITIES FOR PROFESSIONAL RENEWAL

This section described three shifts that leaders can make to lead more like a coach. See Table 1.1 for a visual summary.

Table 1.1 Side-by-Side Comparison of Leading Like a Coach with Traditional School Leadership

Leading Like a Coach	Traditional School Leadership
Co-Developing a Vision for Success	Forming a Goal
Embracing Challenges as Opportunities	Identifying Areas for Improvement
Engaging in Professional Learning	Delivering Professional Development
What else would you add?	

What other areas within your role might have potential for a shift, to leading like a coach? Continue adding to this table on your own in your journal. This shift is mostly mental and largely involves changing how we think and talk about it.

A good place to start is to update your original job description. For example, instead of "exercise fiscal responsibility" when it comes to budgeting duties, we can reimagine this as "prioritize and invest in sound educational resources." This is a start, and you see where it is going: rethinking our current responsibilities, still honoring some semblance of the original duty, but broadening what is possible in our positions.

NEW WAYS OF TEACHING, LEADING, AND BEING

In my current school, students lead building tours for guests. I provide some initial training, with them following me during a tour and observing the process.

The students are so good at guiding our guests. During the tours, they can remember aspects of former classrooms as if they were there yesterday. "And in this corner of the preschool room, it used to be the ice-skating rink and the ice was wax paper." Teachers feel affirmed and guests are impressed. These are perspectives of our school that I do not have, that only students and their teachers can recall and talk about with clarity.

Part of releasing the responsibility of school tours to students is to have someone fill in when I am absent. But another reason resides in the purpose for education: to prepare our students for an unknown future and a changing world, to provide them with the opportunities to show what they know independently. Visitors see firsthand our students' knowledge and skills. If they make a mistake, it is an opportunity for learning.

In everything we do, we engage in a process that could lead to promising outcomes and whole new identities. And just as the teachers can become more independent and interdependent by leading like a coach, so too can students through our actions and influence.

The primary identity for leaders in this resource, as a coach, becomes more evident in the next chapter as we explore how to engage in new ways of leading through instructional walks in classrooms.

 # Reflective Questions

Consider the following questions to promote reflection. You can respond to them in writing and/or in conversation with colleagues. (I will use the 3-2-1 summary protocol after each chapter.)

1. What are three key takeaways for you after reading this chapter?

2. Of the four specific benefits of leading like a coach, which two did you find most compelling? Why?

3. What one small step could you take today to start building your identity as a coach within your larger role as an instructional leader? How do you think this action might make a difference?

HOW INSTRUCTIONAL WALKS HELP LEADERS ADOPT A COACHING STANCE

Based on a history of principal-as-evaluator, teachers are often wary of this new role, but where principals go in with a respectful stance and a positive viewing lens—and as trust develops—teachers come to welcome their principal as coach, co-teacher, and colleague. Leaders need to first take on the role of supportive coach before taking on the role of evaluator.

—Routman (2014, p. 199)

At my former school, my regular classroom visits were well established. Teachers knew that I was there to simply recognize what was occurring in their practice from an appreciative stance.

A teacher, new to the building but with years of experience elsewhere, was surprised to see me pop in on the second day of a school year.

"Can I help you?" she asked me. "No, please go about your instruction," I responded. "I am here to just sit in and learn." Her quizzical look did not leave her face, but she carried on with instruction.

I later realized that I had not given the new faculty members a heads up on instructional walks and apologized for not communicating my intent. "That's okay," she shared. "It was nice to have someone notice what we are doing in my class and to get some feedback." She confided that in previous school years, she did not even experience an observation from her principal, let alone regular visits.

A leader showing up in classrooms can be more than an event. We best support our teachers with a continuous presence that is both positive and constructive. Instructional walks are how we can engage in this work, in leading like a coach.

INTRODUCING INSTRUCTIONAL WALKS

I encountered this leadership approach in my first school as a head principal. Regie Routman, author of *Read, Write, Lead: Breakthrough Strategies for Schoolwide Literacy Success* (2014), spoke at a literacy leadership institute. She defines "instructional walks" as

> an intentional, informal visit (not an evaluation) by the principal to a teacher's classroom to notice, record, and affirm strengths, build trust, offer possible suggestions, or coach—all for the purpose of increasing student literacy and learning across the curriculum. (p. 306)

While Routman references literacy specifically, instructional walks are applicable to any classroom.

Figure 2.1 is an example of documentation taken during an instructional walk in Jenny Singer's (personal communication, September 4, 2019) fifth-grade classroom. It is a written narrative, a page-long description of the teaching and learning observed, noting and naming what is going well.

Teachers value the affirmation and the feedback about their work. They also see how these visits improve my capacity to lead. As one teacher shared via anonymous feedback, "I appreciate your regular appearances in my classroom. This gives you a good idea of what instruction looks like on a day-to-day basis." It is low stakes and highly collegial.

Figure 2.1 Instructional walk notes: fifth-grade classroom

Jenny – Environment   9-4-19

The students were watching a Brain Pop video about independent and dependent clauses. After the video, the teacher presented a worksheet on the SmartBoard about fragments. "It's the subject, right? 'The dirty sweater' was..." After the explanation, the teacher modeled one of the problems. She then had a student come up and complete another one of the tasks, in front of his peers.

The classroom library was located on the book shelf in the back. Paint sticks were used as location markers, presumably for titles checked out by kids. Some of the books were coded by color; some were not. A variety of genres were offered, fiction and nonfiction, picture books and chapter books. The majority (at first glance) seem to be fiction/chapter book. Comfortable seating in the back corner invited students to read quietly or work together.

Jenny, the furniture you have brought in so far creates a space where students want to be.

Information gained during instructional walks can also be beneficial to our more traditional supervision systems. Current tools for teacher evaluation are not flexible enough for understanding instructional effectiveness. For example, Cohen and Goldhaber (2016) found that the rigidness of evaluation frameworks inhibits leaders' capacity to differentiate their approach when working with teachers in a wide variety of situations.

Related, Hill and Grossman (2013) learned that a leader's content knowledge can positively influence teacher improvement in specific subject areas. Leaders who lack specific content knowledge can help facilitate this process but are often ill-equipped to initially come in and communicate actionable feedback. What they need is significant time in every classroom *to learn*—not judge—which is made possible through instructional walks.

I have observed additional benefits when engaging in this practice.

➤ Documenting and recognizing strong instruction with a nonevaluative, narrative format (my notes) reinforces preferred practices over time.

➤ Focusing first on teachers' strengths opens the door for coaching conversations.

➤ This process of documentation, recognition, and conversation gives teachers consistent opportunities for reflection and improvement.

➤ These more informal experiences "build trust and respect between the principal and teachers" (Routman, 2014, p. 200).

➤ Scanned and saved over time, instructional walk notes help inform opportunities to communicate more constructive feedback for teachers and the entire faculty.

➤ Communicating feedback becomes a reciprocal process; both teachers and leaders learn together.

➤ Leaders who are a positive presence in classrooms are viewed more favorably by students.

➤ Instructional walks are authentic and more closely resemble artifacts collected during a coaching cycle.

THE INSTRUCTIONAL WALK PROCESS

Figure 2.2 is adapted from a process created by Routman (2014).

As you will see in the following examples, the conversation at the end of or shortly after the visit is the key to professional growth. Conversations around practice help both the teacher and the leader construct meaning about what is happening in the classroom. To ensure that my interactions with faculty members are respectful, I utilize three coaching skills (sometimes referred to as "collaborative norms" in the world of Cognitive Coaching).

Figure 2.2 The instructional walk process

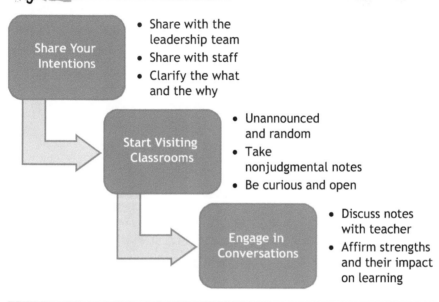

Share Your Intentions
- Share with the leadership team
- Share with staff
- Clarify the what and the why

Start Visiting Classrooms
- Unannounced and random
- Take nonjudgmental notes
- Be curious and open

Engage in Conversations
- Discuss notes with teacher
- Affirm strengths and their impact on learning

COACHING COLLABORATIVE NORMS

1. *Paraphrasing*: Restating what the other person said the way you heard it

2. *Posing Questions*: Sharing aloud what we are wondering or would like to clarify

3. *Pausing*: Waiting silently to give time for everyone to process their thinking

My conversations with teachers, supported by these coaching skills, typically last three to five minutes. They are guided by what was just observed, documented in my notes.

On paper, instructional walks may appear easy to implement. Grab a notepad plus a pen and walk around the school. Go into classrooms, selecting a few to sit in and write down observations. Share your notes with the teacher and engage in a coaching conversation.

In reality, our days are filled with responsibilities calling for our attention. Instructional walks aren't "required," so we may tend to push them off to the next day. Maybe we don't see immediate results, such as with a traditional walkthrough where you can tick off boxes when elements of instruction are observed.

That is why committing to daily instructional walks is key. To help make this process a regular part of my schedule, I have found a few helpful strategies.

HELPFUL STRATEGIES FOR MAKING INSTRUCTIONAL WALKS ROUTINE

- *Identify the benefits of regular classroom visits:* What are your reasons for spending time with students and teachers? For example, we can see teaching and learning in action without worrying about evaluation. Additionally, students and staff appreciate our visibility in the school.

- *Remember the "why" of this approach:* For me, it is always about supporting our journey toward schoolwide excellence, and ensuring that every student has access to a great education. We are playing the long game. The only way to know we are on the right pathway toward our long-term goals is by showing up every day.

- *Set yourself up with the right tools:* Everyone is different, but I prefer low to no technology. A padfolio with paper and a pen is all I need. Not including technology during instructional walks, when possible, helps me differentiate these visits from formal observations for teachers, in which a laptop is usually involved. In addition, I am less distracted when I do not have a screen and all its notifications in front of me.

One of the best benefits of the instructional walk process is hearing what the kids have to say. I like to sit adjacent to students, adopting a learner's stance to "see" instruction from a student's perspective. After conducting instructional walks regularly, students barely notice you, especially if they are deeply engaged in their learning. This is often when you can capture your best observations as the experiences are authentic.

I recall sitting in a primary classroom while students were playing math games. One group started to struggle with setting the game up, such as who goes first. The teacher came over to assess the situation. Once the students explained the problem, the teacher asked, "So what can we do to fix this?" A long pause, then one student came up with a suggestion. The teacher provided time for the group to process this idea, then asked, "What do you all think? Would this work?" The kids looked at each other and nodded. The teacher did not stop there. "Did you notice how we solved this problem? What did we do to be successful?" The students and the teacher listed several strategies they used, such as asking questions and listening to each other's ideas.

Once I finished transcribing this conversation, I handed over my notes to the teacher and shared the following:

> You aren't just reinforcing math skills; you are also teaching your students how to collaboratively solve problems. That is a skill they can use in any subject area and in many walks of life. You are developing thoughtful and empathetic individuals.

She thanked me for noticing. "It is hard to take more time for that type of teaching, but so worth it for building a positive learning community," she replied.

This is the reward we receive when we show up without an agenda and instead allow instruction to guide our observations and subsequent conversations. When we take a learning stance, we see powerful instruction in places we might not expect it. With instructional walks, we surface promising practices that are often invisible during formal observations.

ACTIVITY 2.1 — START WITH CELEBRATION

Teaching and leading is stressful. One gift we can give our faculty and ourselves is to recognize the positive practices and noteworthy efforts every day. In many residencies conducted in the United States and Canada, Routman (2014) has found that "celebration is at the heart of all effective teaching and learning" (p. 186). She defines celebration as when "we honestly let the learner know, whether it's a teacher or a student, exactly what he or she has done well or attempted to do" (p. 186).

By starting with celebration, we become partners in the teaching and learning experience. This initial approach is a critical strategy for initiating conversations around our practices versus being in constant evaluation mode or delivering blanket praise. As Routman (2014) notes, "celebration must come before evaluation if teachers are to value and benefit from formal evaluations" (p. 186). Trust and relationships need to be established between the leader and the teacher for more constructive feedback to be communicated.

(Continued)

(Continued)

One way to celebrate is using handwritten notes or annotated images of instruction. Regarding notes, I purchase personalized stationery pads with my name and contact information. As I walk through classrooms in the beginning of the year, I have one of these pads on hand. When I see high-quality practices or a genuine attempt at a new instructional strategy, I will commend their efforts with a short note in their mailbox. Figure 2.3 is one example, which I gave to kindergarten teacher Jill McGuire.

Figure 2.3 **Celebrate promising practices with notes of affirmation**

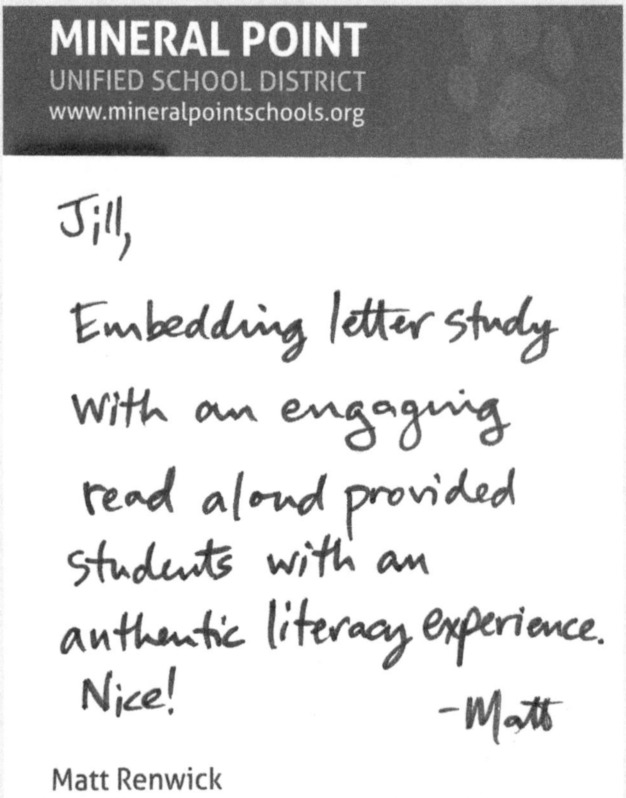

MINERAL POINT
UNIFIED SCHOOL DISTRICT
www.mineralpointschools.org

Jill,

Embedding letter study
with an engaging
read aloud provided
students with an
authentic literacy experience.
Nice!
    —Matt

Matt Renwick

Consider trying this in your school. Start noting and naming what's going well in classrooms. You will find that teachers will treasure these recognitions, pinning them on their corkboards and saving to reread later. In addition, you will start to feel a similar sense of appreciation. Gratitude benefits both the recipient and the messenger.

While celebration is essential for building trust and self-confidence, it is also only the first step toward continuous improvement. Conversations among educators are what foster the greatest amount of professional growth. For instance, Hiebert and Stigler (2017) compared lesson study in Japan with the U.S. approach to professional development. They found that collaborative discussions focused on *teaching*—instead of *teachers*—led to improved theories about effective instruction, a more aligned and adaptive curriculum, and a better sense of professionalism among faculty. More promising practices dispersed throughout the school. All results were associated with improved academic outcomes.

This type of culture begins when we adopt a coaching stance via instructional walks. When we shift to a learning stance, we renew our purpose for classroom visits, from "How are we doing?" to "What are we doing, why are we doing it, and how is it making a difference?"

MAKE INSTRUCTIONAL WALKS A HABIT

If we only rely on reminders and willpower to engage in daily classroom visits, they may never become a consistent part of our practice. This is why I suggest developing a habit with instructional walks.

The science of habit formation is well documented. Bestselling books by Duhigg (2012) and Fogg (2020) have summarized the process for creating a habit:

1. *Cue or prompt:* an antecedent that triggers a response

2. *Action or routine:* the response prompted by the cue

3. *Celebration or reward:* a positive, intentional act immediately after the response

A personal example: When starting this book, I had to develop a better writing habit. Prior, I would find time after school or in between dinner and going to bed. Sometimes family experiences were missed. So my habit involved a morning writing routine. I now wake up earlier than I have in the past, commit to writing for at least 20 minutes, and then reward myself with some quiet time, a cup of coffee, and reflective journaling.

Here is my writing habit:

1. *Cue/prompt:* the alarm

2. *Action/routine:* write for 20 minutes

3. *Celebration/reward:* quiet time to think and reflect

This same process can be applied to instructional walks. Here is how I have set up this habit; you can use the same approach.

1. *Cue/prompt:* At the beginning of each week, I schedule 1.5 hours to visit classrooms. I set these appointments in my Google Calendar at specific times to ensure that I am getting a full understanding of collective instruction. The cue is the appointment reminder going off on my computer and my phone 10 minutes prior.

2. *Action/routine:* I select two or three rooms to conduct an instructional walk. I carry a checklist to ensure that I am conducting walks for all teachers.

3. *Celebration/reward:* When I hand over my notes to the teacher, accompanied by recognition, I feel good. The smile on the teacher's face and beams of pride from the students when I share my observations tell me they appreciate the acknowledgment. In addition, I also check off that teacher's name, giving me a sense of accomplishment.

How will you know if instructional walks have become a habit? One indicator is you start to feel "off" when you are not going into classrooms. It is your mind telling you that it wants to affirm and support others, and that it has associated this feeling with instructional walks.

Another indicator is other people will notice when you are not engaging in your habit. Now, during the rare time I do not wake up early before the rest of my family, my wife will ask me why I am not writing today. A similar thing occurs with instructional walks; teachers will comment that they have not seen you in a while. Students will ask when you are coming to their classroom again.

BUILD AN INSTRUCTIONAL WALK HABIT

Plan to conduct "*x*" number of instructional walks next week.

- Block off the time in your digital calendar and create a notification as a cue.

- Spend at least 25% of your day visiting all classrooms and select two or three of those classrooms per day to observe, document, and celebrate. This results in high-quality instructional walkthroughs in about 10 to 15 classrooms per week.

- Journal afterward. How did the walks make you feel? What went well? What would you do differently next time? Celebrate your efforts and the positive actions you noticed.

WISDOM FROM THE FIELD: ACT LIKE A RESEARCHER

It took instructional coach Sam Bennett between 30 and 40 classroom visits (about 4 years) before she was able to ask high school English teacher and author Cris Tovani a question that caused her to rethink her instruction. This question came in the form of a "coaching letter." Cris still has this letter. Sam "acted like a researcher" in her early visits to learn as much as she could about Cris's highly respected work (Bennett & Tovani, 2020).

Think about the experienced and highly effective teachers in your school. How many times do you estimate you will need to visit their classroom and learn before you might generate a question that may highlight an area for improvement? How might you act like a researcher? Jot down your ideas and thoughts in your journal.

FROM JUDGING TO LEARNING

When I first started as a head principal in 2012, I was skeptical of instructional walks. Quietly, I raised several questions and concerns to myself:

➤ *I already do teacher observations—isn't this redundant?*

➤ *I do not have enough time in the day for one more thing.*

➤ *Teachers will feel uncomfortable with me popping in their classrooms unannounced.*

So I put instructional walks on the backburner at the time. Today I am engaged daily in instructional walks, regularly visiting classrooms and experiencing instruction. What changed, and why did the change take so long?

As previous studies shared have shown, the teacher evaluation process by itself may not facilitate professional growth. I do see merits of the system, such as accountability when addressing poor performance. Specific indicators of practice under domains such as "Instructional Delivery" and "Assessment of and for Learning" provide clarity and objectivity when principals observe teachers. It is an improvement on previous systems, such as when a supervisor would pop in and write a qualitative narrative of instruction through their subjective point of view.

However, current supervision systems are *evaluative by design*. We are asked for our judgment about a teacher's performance. If the information collected from an observation is used to make decisions about one's performance and possibly their employment status, how can it also foster growth?

With that, consider the following two examples from my school to appreciate how instructional walks can help create clarity, as well as opportunities for coaching conversations around the classroom experience. When we focus first on strengths and lead with curiosity, we can better see all the good that is happening in our schools.

> *Current supervision systems are evaluative by design. We are asked for our judgment about a teacher's performance. If the information collected from an observation is used to make decisions about one's performance and possibly their employment status, how can it also foster growth?*

EXAMPLE 2.1: BOOK CLUBS WITH MIDDLE SCHOOL STUDENTS

Instructional walks offer a responsive and authentic approach to continuous professional development for all educators. This development includes principals. I have learned at least as much if not more from many of the teachers I have connected with during my regular classroom visits. Until instructional walks became a priority, my background in literacy was limited to the resources I pulled in while teaching full-time.

For example, during an instructional walk in an online middle-level classroom co-taught by Dalton Miles and Kris McCoy, I observed students discussing the books they were reading for their clubs. Within the videoconferencing tool, they would take turns sharing their thinking about what they had previously read, prompted by their teachers.

As the group transitioned to a whole-group reading strategy lesson, I thought to myself, *"The teachers devoted significant time for students to share their understanding. Would it have been more efficient to give a quick quiz?"* This thinking was partially based on this new platform (Zoom); instruction seems to require more time when online. Yet I knew my role was not to judge but to notice what was occurring through an appreciative lens. So I continued to observe as the teachers demonstrated their thinking processes for one of the books they were reading.

Later, I emailed my notes to the teachers, acknowledging the opportunity provided for students to share their understanding of what they had read so far. I also wondered why they devoted that amount of time to check for understanding.

Through our conversation, I learned that public check-ins help everyone construct meaning about the text. In addition, the teachers would use their responses as teaching opportunities. For example, a student shared their observation from *Legend* by Marie Lu that mortality rates were high in their science fiction story. Mr. Miles responded, "Things aren't great in this dystopian American society." This follow-up affirmed the student's thinking *and* included genre-specific terms in the discussion for the group to hear.

(Continued)

(Continued)

My initial belief was to maximize instructional time in the form of direct teaching and brief assessments. What I learned is that giving students the opportunity to share their thinking about their books *is* instructional time. The teachers' responsive approach to facilitating conversations around books also encouraged them to identify as readers.

With an open mind during the walk, my understanding improved. I remembered the importance of assuming a teacher believes they are doing the best they can for their students, and then recognized the authentic environment they created for readers.

Had I come into the classroom with only my preexisting thinking about reading instruction (which does not include any experience teaching these grades), our conversation may not have led to a better understanding on my end, nor the teachers affirmed in their practice. Our conversation around their decision-making was supported by my curiosity.

SPECIAL NOTE: INSTRUCTIONAL WALKS AND VIRTUAL INSTRUCTION

The previous example highlights how leading like a coach might look within virtual instruction. As of this writing, the pandemic that began in 2020 is still influencing how education is facilitated. Teaching in online spaces will continue beyond the resolution of this major global event.

During the 2020-2021 school year, I engaged in instructional walks in two ways when our school was virtual: observing live instruction via a digital conferencing tool like Zoom or watching a recorded video of instruction. Both approaches worked for affirming what teachers were doing well and communicating constructive feedback.

I did make a few adjustments to accommodate these situations:

- For live virtual instruction (also known as synchronous), instead of writing a narrative I summarized the key events from the lesson in a bulleted list. In the margins, I wrote my affirmations and questions about what I was observing. These notes were discussed after the lesson and emailed to the teachers as a scanned copy.

- For instruction that already occurred and was recorded, I followed the more traditional instructional walk process of a written observational narrative and ended with some summarizing thoughts. I had time to pause the video and reread what I wrote before posing any questions or possible next steps.

A challenge that I did not encounter was asynchronous instruction. This is when learning tasks, assessments, and student discussions are hosted in a learning management system (LMS) like Canvas and Schoology. Students can engage in learning when it works best for them. If I were to lead more like a coach in these situations, I would likely conference with the teacher as we explored the LMS together, focused on one aspect of their instruction in which they would appreciate another perspective.

EXAMPLE 2.2: SHARED READING IN FOURTH GRADE

I was sitting near the back of a fourth-grade classroom, next to the classroom library. The students and the teacher, Livia Doyle (personal communication, February 3, 2020), were engaged in a shared reading of a historical fiction novel. While the students followed along in their copy of the book as the teacher read aloud, my mind was making assumptions about whole-class novel studies.

- *They are teacher-directed and do not provide for student voice and choice.*
- *One common text does not address different reading abilities.*
- *Time spent reading together means less time reading independently.*

Fortunately, I stopped that line of thinking and simply observed. After a few minutes, Livia paused where she was reading and asked the students to turn and talk about the story so far. Then she walked over to where I was sitting and shared, "We are using this novel to teach students how to have authentic conversations about what they are reading. We are starting with turn and talk. Gradually we will build in roles and more strategies."

I thanked her for sharing this information with me. Our school goal at the time was "A Community of Readers." The teacher was taking a text they use within their study of history and implementing discussion strategies we were learning about during professional development. I added this context to the anecdotal notes I was writing before giving them to Livia. My notes, shown in Figure 2.4, were accompanied by my public comment about how engaged everyone seemed to be in their conversations around the text.

Figure 2.4 **Document what you learned from your teachers**

> Livia, OLM Application   11-26-18
>
> "Can't you just picture that in your
> mind?" The teacher was reading
> aloud Little House/the Big Woods as a
> shared reading aloud with the whole class.
> "We are pretty far into the chapter and
> it's a long one. Please get together in
> groups of three or four to read together
> and talk some more about the book.
> Students in one group assigned each other
> a passage, and then one of them began
> reading aloud for the group.
>
> The teacher walked around the classroom,
> checking in on where a group was location-
> wise and they could successfully begin. "It's
> the same exact text, just formatted differently."
> The teacher gave one student her copy so
> he could better follow along with the group.
> This was the beginning of an historical
> fiction unit, practicing literature circle roles.
>
> Livia, thanks for sharing how you are
> scaffolding the literacy activity to ensure
> all students are successful readers. I enjoyed
> watching the OLM in action.

In both the examples, *it was I who initially needed the coaching*. This learning occurred because the teachers knew of my intentions: not to evaluate or to judge, but to be present and to understand so that I became more knowledgeable to better support their practice. This openness to the experience is the entry point to future dialogue about their instruction.

WHAT INSTRUCTIONAL WALKS ARE NOT

Clarity is key for this work, both for leaders and for the faculty. If teachers do not understand why we are coming into classrooms and leaving notes, we may be creating confusion.

How are instructional walks different from other instructional leadership actions? Here are some of the most common approaches and how they compare/contrast with instructional walks.

MINI-OBSERVATIONS

These unannounced visits to classrooms are a shorter version of traditional observations. They are still part of a teacher evaluation system. Marshall (2013) advocates for this approach and discourages longer, announced formal observations. The advantage of the former is leaders get into classrooms more frequently and yield more evidence of instruction. Yet all observations, full or mini, are evaluative.

▶ *How instructional walks are different:* Instructional walks avoid judgment. Leaders are there to document the experience, to support strong instruction, and to facilitate reflection on practice. Because instructional walks are focused on strengths first and naturally lead to coaching conversations, I have found they more often support professional growth through dialogue and reflection. Teacher supervision consultants Danielson (2016) and Stronge (2019) have also acknowledged the limits of formal evaluations. It is a similar distinction between formative assessment (assessment *for* learning) and summative assessment (assessment *of* learning). Building trusting relationships between leaders and teachers is better facilitated through low-stakes experiences.

ROUNDS

This approach to observing instruction involves a group of educators walking through classrooms and documenting what is occurring, looking for patterns and trends about instruction in a school. Two types of rounds are "teacher rounds" (Del Prete, 2013) and "instructional rounds" (City et al., 2009). They are based on the medical model of rounds that teams of doctors make with patients. The goal is teachers or administrators capturing data around a problem of practice. This information is then analyzed to inform school improvement plans and adjust future professional learning.

▶ *How instructional walks are different:* The learning that occurs during instructional walks is between the teacher and the leader. There is a mutual benefit: the teacher gets feedback on their current practice, and the leader learns about the instruction occurring in their school. Through subsequent dialogue and more visits, a host of benefits already discussed are realized. With rounds, the learning that occurs is primarily with the observers and less with the observed. Additionally, trust and relationships are developed during instructional walks. Having the principal be a regular presence in classrooms resets the mindset of administrator as only an evaluator; we are now able to mentor or coach.

WALKTHROUGHS

Similar to instructional rounds, walkthroughs are short visits to classrooms with the purpose of collecting information about instruction in a building. Leaders observe one aspect of instructional practice with the larger goal of understanding the general status of teaching and learning in a school. Yet walkthroughs can involve many things depending on who is asked. The classroom data collected could be quantitative or qualitative. The visits could be formative or evaluative. Feedback might come from the observer during or after instruction, or not at all. The focus for the walkthroughs could be tightly aligned with standards or loosely defined regarding quality of instruction. This lack of clarity can lead to negligible or even negative outcomes from our visits, especially if teachers are left with little, no, or inaccurate feedback. As former principal and leadership consultant DeWitt (2020) notes, "walkthroughs, when implemented without deep thought and planning, can do more harm than good" (p. 30).

▶ *How instructional walks are different*: While it is hard to pin down one definition for walkthroughs, instructional walks are clear. The goal is to celebrate and improve instruction schoolwide. This occurs through the process itself. Instructional walks provide a starting point for authentic conversation around practice. As Routman (2014) notes, "we are not just quietly observing and writing notes the teacher may or may not see, checking off look-fors, or collecting numerical data through a clicker. It is a process that respects both teacher and students" (p. 200). Instructional walks are centered on supporting the teacher and the students. Teachers know the purpose of this practice and how it benefits everyone involved.

To be clear, formal observations can serve as an important accountability tool, especially for documenting ineffective instruction. Rounds and walkthroughs can capture data about instruction efficiently to examine progress toward schoolwide goals. But we also need to be aware about their limitations. Teaching and learning is complex. Observations and walkthroughs tend to distill instruction down to a level or a score, dependent on the observer with little insight from the observed. Yet can we say with 100% certainty what effect any instructional task has on a student? Cohen et al. (2020) found that formal observations cannot capture the intricacies of classroom instruction due to the general nature of evaluation rubric language. These tools are implemented with every classroom in mind, which means they can miss what makes every classroom unique and special.

To summarize, it is not the documentation of classroom instruction, but the subsequent dialogue and reflection made possible through the instructional walk process where we collectively improve the teaching and learning in our schools. Leaving these preferred outcomes to chance, such as by assuming that walkthroughs, formal observations, or instructional rounds will serve this purpose, may at best maintain the status quo.

People improve in environments more conducive to growth. Instructional walks and professional conversations enrich a community like no other supervisory practice.

> *Teaching and learning is complex. Observations and walkthroughs tend to distill instruction down to a level or a score, dependent on the observer with little insight from the observed. Yet can we say with 100% certainty what effect any instructional task has on a student?*

INSTRUCTIONAL LEADERSHIP IN ACTION

For decades, professionals in education have tried to define "instructional leadership." The purpose is to develop a clear understanding of what it is leaders do to improve teaching and learning in schools. Next are a few of the most recent definitions.

Instructional leadership is . . .

When those in a leadership position focus on implementing practices that will increase student learning.

—DeWitt (2020, p. 10)

The practice of making and implementing operational and improvement decisions.

—Baeder (2018, p. 2)

Phillip Hallinger, a pioneer in instructional leadership, offers a framework for this concept using three categories:

1. Create the school mission.
2. Manage the instructional program.
3. Develop a positive school learning climate.

—Hallinger et al. (2018)

Yet what does this look like in action? Where do we start? How do we know if we are successful? This is the purpose for the rest of this book: to share specific strategies for engaging in leadership actions that will lead to instructional improvement.

We do this by following the C.O.A.C.H. framework, a pathway toward schoolwide success, and by engaging in instructional walks every day. See the bulleted list for how the tenets of instructional leadership are embedded in this approach and this practice:

- By *creating confidence through trust*, such as through developing the collaborative norms for how we talk and listen with each other, we *develop a positive school learning climate* for everyone.

- By *organizing around a priority*, for example, identifying a high-leverage instructional strategy to learn about and apply to our collective practice, we create alignment between *the district's mission and vision* and classroom instruction.

- By *affirming promising practices* to validate and encourage what is already working in our school, and by *communicating feedback* with teachers to support continuous improvement, we *manage the instructional program* by implementing what we believe is most effective for student learning.

- By consistently engaging in the first four practices, we are *helping teachers become leaders and learners*. We co-create a collective belief that a community of professionals can make a real and positive impact on the lives of their students. The true role of a school leader is then realized: uncovering the potential of a school that was there from the beginning.

 # Reflective Questions

Consider the following questions to promote reflection. You can respond to them in writing and/or in conversation with colleagues.

1. What are three key takeaways for you after reading this chapter?

2. Think about each of your faculty members. Which two teachers do you think would be most open to having you conduct initial instructional walks in their classrooms? Why?

3. What one habit could you drop and replace with instructional walks? For example, do you need to check email as frequently as you currently do? How much time might you recapture for classroom visits if digital messaging was scheduled for only a couple of times a day?

CREATE CONFIDENCE THROUGH TRUST

Trust serves as a lubricant of organizational functioning; without it, schools are likely to experience the overheated friction of conflict as well as a lack of progress toward their admirable goals.

—Tschannen-Moran (2014, p. ix)

One year in my school, I attempted to start a lending library in our staff lounge. Books were brought from home to outfit the four shelves beneath the staff mailboxes. The space did not get much attention, possibly because it was *my* project. I didn't ask for help or input. I also did not invest in the space either—only secondhand books.

I found an idea in *Becoming a Literacy Leader* by Jennifer Allen (2016): purchase a gift card to a physical bookstore and have teacher leaders select titles the staff would want available. After a trip to the bookstore, three of our teachers outfitted the lending library with many new books by authors such as Jacqueline Woodson, Ruta Sepetys, Chris Cleave, Amy Bright, and Herman Koch.

My wife, who works in my building, saw this space and immediately grabbed *Where the Crawdads Sing* by Delia Owens. As soon as she was done reading it, another teacher snagged it, read it, and then left a sticky note on the cover with her short recommendation.

This was a small yet formative experience with trust. I let go of my desire to control the outcomes of this project and placed faith in my faculty members to carry it out. With this trust was a transfer of power.

Leaders' beliefs are realized in their actions. Too often our actions convey a lack of trust throughout our profession. It is not necessarily intentional; so much responsibility is thrust on administrators by external and internal parties. Yet this lack of belief in teachers' capacity to improve has resulted in low confidence in ourselves and is subsequently perceived this way by others. For example, the American Enterprise Institute released a report titled, "Still Left Behind: How America's Schools Keep Failing Our Children" (Stevens & Tracy, 2020). Reports with titles like this promote the narrative that educators alone are to be blamed for lagging test scores rather than inadequate funding, understaffing, disparities in family income and parents' education levels, and biased standardized tests.

Leaders' beliefs are realized in their actions.

This is a no-win, low-confidence situation. People cannot become trustworthy unless someone offers them the opportunity and the support to do so. This is the first and the foundational principle for leading like a coach: creating confidence through trust.

DEFINING TRUST

Professor and former principal Megan Tschannen-Moran (2014) defines trust as "the willingness to be vulnerable to another based on the confidence that the other is benevolent, honest, open, reliable, and competent" (pp. 19-20).

Trust is the bedrock for all leadership efforts. Without it, all subsequent actions toward improving instruction through professional learning fail to take hold. As Routman (2014) notes, "when trust is missing, fear is often present, and fear is a guaranteed antidote to learning" (p. 20).

For example, indicators of a negative school climate such as teachers' intent to leave are decreased when trust-supporting actions are implemented by leaders (Qadach et al., 2020). Developing structures for professional dialogue and involving teachers in schoolwide decision-making help foster a sense of belonging among staff. They believe their input matters and is valued.

In another study that examined instructional leadership actions of principals, the determining factor of successful schools was the level of trust the teachers had in their leader (Ma & Marion, 2021). Trust enhanced faculty members' understanding of the school's goals and the implementation of preferred instructional practices. School climate is also more positive when teachers find their leader trustworthy.

So how is trust essential for leading like a coach? Because when we release the responsibility for learning outcomes to teachers and students, as well as highlight their successes through instructional walks and coaching conversations, we build confidence.

In other words, to create the conditions for trust, we as leaders must exhibit behaviors that convey that our teachers are capable—that we believe they are trustworthy. It is what Tschannen-Moran (2014) refers to as a "leap of faith." We are confident that our faculty can facilitate student learning, and through our positive support they meet these expectations.

So how do we build trust and increase confidence? Four conditions in place can help ensure success.

FOUR CONDITIONS FOR TRUST

Building trust takes time and patience, as well as a common language so people can talk about this construct. Where do we begin?

In a review of the literature and research on trust, Vodicka (2006) discovered and defined four conditions that comprise trust in schools: consistency, compassion, communication, and competency.

FOUR CONDITIONS OF TRUST IN SCHOOLS

1. *Consistency*: The messages for different audiences—parents, staff members, students, and the community—carry the same meaning.

2. *Compassion*: The act of caring for another; in a relationship, it implies there is a semblance of protection, and that one person will not do harm to the other person.

3. *Communication*: Citing other researchers, Vodicka characterizes communication as offering and requesting feedback on performance within safe conditions.

4. *Competence*: Displaying and counting on one another to complete a task with efficiency and efficacy.

When these four conditions are present, schools can expect the following outcomes:

- A more positive school climate
- An increased orientation to innovation
- Improved collaboration among faculty (Vodicka, 2006)

High levels of trust also have academic benefits. In one study, "schools with high levels of trust between school professionals and parents, between teachers and the principal, and among teachers were *three times more likely to improve in reading and mathematics* than those schools with low levels of trust" (Bryk & Schneider, 2002, my emphasis).

To initiate the development of trust, it starts with us as leaders.

To initiate the development of trust, it starts with us as leaders. In one study that Vodicka (2006) reviewed, "how much teachers trust their principal is wholly dependent on the behaviors of the principal" (p. 28). In other words, we must take that first step in developing positive relationships with each of our faculty members.

Building trust may take years to establish and sustain. Yet teachers deserve our faith in their capacity to change. We have no crystal ball, so let us assume renewal is possible.

An example: In one school where literacy consultant Routman (2014) had led several weeklong professional learning residencies, a reluctant teacher finally shared his thoughts aloud during a whole faculty discussion. When she asked him what took so long to contribute, he responded, "I've been watching you. I had to be sure I could trust you" (p. 21). Routman noted that this was their third year of working together and that the teacher's students finally began to make modest gains because he had started participating in the professional learning and trying some of the ideas in his classroom.

When we convey trust, we communicate "I believe in you" and "You can do this." The rest of this chapter describes specific actions leaders can take to foster these four conditions. Our end goal is to create a sustainable, self-directed school of leaders and learners. We begin by shifting some of the power to where it belongs: with the teachers and the students in the classroom.

ACTIVITY 3.1 — ANALYZE YOUR INSTRUCTIONAL EXPERIENCE

I have conducted this exercise with leaders during workshops, to help them understand how limited our experience is in our respective schools. This activity gives us perspective and helps us understand how important it is that we trust in and learn with our teachers.

1. Draw a table.
2. Include a row for every grade level or subject area taught in your school.
3. Add columns representing years of teaching experience.
4. Put an "X" in the box for the number of years teaching in a grade level or subject area.

Here is what my table looks like.

Grade level	Years of teaching experience						
	1	2	3	4	5	6	7
4-year-old kindergarten							
Kindergarten							
Grade 1							
Grade 2							
Grade 3	X						
Grade 4	X						
Grade 5						X	

As you can see, I have one year of teaching in grades 3 and 4, and six years of teaching in grade 5. I have no experience teaching at the primary level. What this tells me is I have much to learn, and that the teachers in most of our classrooms likely hold considerably more knowledge about instruction at their level. Trusting our teachers in their instructional decision-making is what leading like a coach is all about.

- What did you discover from this exercise?
- Where do you have much to learn?
- What are ways that you can serve as a coach to teachers who have more teaching experience than you in a certain grade or subject area?

CONDITION 1: CONSISTENCY

Students benefit from consistency. This goes for professionals too. Being consistent, such as through daily and nonjudgmental classroom visits, helps others predict the future. A sense of knowing what is likely to come reduces anxiety and increases confidence.

Consistency is not by itself a trust builder. (Devin Vodicka recommends that all four conditions of trust—consistency, compassion, communication, and competence—be present at the same time.) As leaders, we want to aim for the kind of predictability that effectively supports teachers and students. This requires understanding how we are perceived by staff when we speak, communicate information, and act. The following practices can help you achieve greater consistency.

Collective Commitments

To build a trusting environment, a school can develop collective commitments. Collective commitments define our beliefs and values, how we behave, and what we know to be true (DuFour et al., 2016).

In my first year at my current school, I invited interested teachers to help craft statements as potential collective commitments. Relevant professional articles were read prior to help initiate the process. Here are the seven statements we crafted together and presented to our colleagues for consideration.

Our Collective Commitments:
What a Trusting School Looks Like

1. I will be open to and ready for learning from others as professionals and colleagues.

2. I will hear others' ideas in various learning communities and be willing to try a variety of practices.

3. I will assume best intentions in our colleagues (positive presupposition) and help create a sense of belonging.

4. I will honor the whole child by treating them with respect and care and attend to their social and emotional needs.

5. I will listen to the concerns of our students' families, address their needs to the best extent possible, and make them feel welcome in the school.

6. I will utilize more promising practices to deliver a coherent and relevant curriculum across all grade levels.

7. I will hold all students to high academic and behavioral expectations regardless of background, label, or past experiences.

To ensure agreement around the commitments, I asked teachers to respond to each statement with a rating of 1 to 5, with a 1 being

"I cannot commit to this statement," a 3 being "I am fine with this statement," and a 5 being "I will champion this statement." If the average for each commitment was a 3 or above, we considered that consensus. We did not need everyone to be a 5, but we did need everyone to have input and know they could live with these commitments. (We did accept all commitments as written.)

These commitments are now referenced during staff meetings and classroom visits. They provide parameters for the work. For example, when I noticed a teacher guiding students to set their own learning goals, I asked her how she learned about this promising practice (Collective Commitments 1 and 6).

These commitments also give educators a common language when engaging in any professional dialogue, whether they are formal collaborations or informal conversations in the hallway. If someone's words or actions stray from these agreements, we can reference them to redirect any discussion that might be less than professional. But this is easier said than done, which is why schools also need collaborative norms to achieve consistency.

Collaborative Norms

If collective commitments describe *what* a trusting school looks and sounds like, then collaborative norms define *how* people convey trustworthiness. Collaborative norms are coaching skills: ways of listening, responding to one another, and sharing ideas productively. These actions help professionals open lines for successful communication.

> If collective commitments describe what a trusting school looks and sounds like, then collaborative norms define how people convey trustworthiness.

The collaborative norms we use in our school come from the world of Cognitive Coaching (Costa et al., 2016).

Our Collaborative Norms: How
We Will Convey Trustworthiness

1. *Pausing:* To provide wait time/silence for the other person to think and to process their thinking

2. *Paraphrasing:* To restate what the other person said in the way you heard what was shared

3. *Posing Questions:* To ask questions to clarify what is shared, to cause someone to think differently about the situation, or to reflect on an experience

4. *Putting Ideas on the Table:* To offer suggestions to choose from for next steps

5. *Providing Data:* To share information from an experience as evidence for analysis, evaluation, and reflection

6. *Paying Attention to Self and Others:* To be mindful about our own actions, language, and thoughts as well as others' actions and language

7. *Presuming Positive Intentions:* To assume someone's actions come from a positive place

The first three norms—pausing, paraphrasing, posing questions—are the key coaching skills to utilize in our interactions with others. These three norms can be thought of as the legs for a stool that supports our larger goal: engaged listening. This concept is summarized in Figure 3.1.

Figure 3.1   Engaging listening/key coaching skills

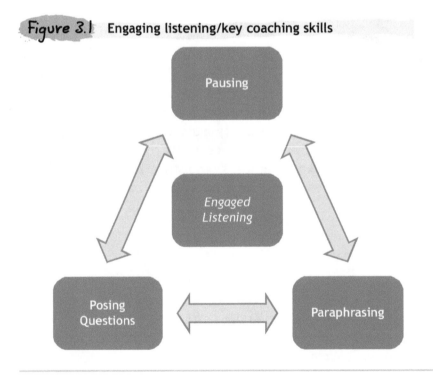

What do these collaborative norms look like in action? Next is a series of interactions between a teacher and me that took place during informal classroom visits in his freshman English class. In this first step, I engage with the teacher by simply being present to his questions and ideas. (*Note:* This is from my first year in administration, as a secondary level assistant principal. What I could not remember specifically, I had to "invent the truth" [Zinsser, 1998] as I recalled this experience. Additionally, I was not using instructional walks formally, but I did engage in coaching conversations with teachers.)

EXAMPLE 3.1: BEING PRESENT TO DISCUSS PRACTICE AND POSSIBILITIES

We were engaged in our first professional learning session as a whole faculty. The teachers were exploring the book *Classroom Instruction That Works* by Marzano et al. (2001). This text had been selected by the leadership team for the school, made up of department heads. The teacher leaders decided to focus on three instructional strategies per year over the course of three years (there were a total of nine). Our school's vision was aligned with this commitment: to employ teaching practices with evidence that they could lead to improved student learning.

After reviewing our norms for professional dialogue, the facilitator for the session gave each group time to discuss the information that was just presented. My table neighbor and freshman English teacher Jason asked me what I thought about these ideas. "There seems to be a lot of research to support the practices, and nothing here really surprises me as being effective." We chatted more about one of the strategies of focus, "Nonlinguistic Representations."

Agreeing that graphic organizers could be helpful for Jason's students to monitor their thinking while reading and organize their writing, he shared that he would start with this instructional strategy in the fall. "That sounds like a great plan—start small and experience some success. Let me know if I can be of help."

SPECIAL NOTE: THE ROLE OF TECHNOLOGY WHEN SUPERVISING INSTRUCTION

During my first attempts with instruction walks, I used an iPad, a stylus, and a notetaking application. There was a convenience found in saving my digitized notes in the cloud and emailing my observations to the teacher. However, I found myself more focused on notetaking and less attentive to fostering professional rapport. In addition, the

(Continued)

teachers were sometimes unsure if my visits were instructional walks or formal observations because of the technology present. (I always use a computer when observing instruction as part of our teacher evaluation process.) The technology may have been undermining the trust I was trying to build with faculty.

On reflection, I went back to handwriting my observational notes and then physically handing them to the teacher after scanning them in with a smartphone app (Evernote, www.evernote.com). Physically handing over my notes to the teacher reminded me to engage in a conversation with the teacher about their instruction, which over time led to increased confidence in asking follow-up questions and offering constructive feedback for possible improvement.

CONDITION 2: COMPASSION

> Personal trust precedes professional trust and is its foundation.
>
> —Routman (2014, p. 22)

Within the construct of trust, compassion can be defined as demonstrating a sense of understanding for others and showing that we care. This is different from empathy in which we understand another person's situation and feelings. With compassion, we act on this awareness with a desire to make things better.

Like consistency, demonstrating compassionate behaviors involves both what we do and what we say. Compassion is an act of caring, "expressing support for one another in a variety of ways across both the professional and personal realms of life" (Tschannen-Moran, 2014, p. 129). Knowing we are cared for and understood is also a confidence booster; people engaged in learning within these conditions of trust will innovate and take more risks.

Convey a Sense of Caring

There are many ways we can show compassion. If it is thoughtful and genuine, simple gestures can make a difference in fostering trust schoolwide.

Recognize Accomplishments Publicly and Regularly

We want to reinforce positive actions and steps taken toward our desired goal. Celebrating people's efforts and accomplishments offers a model for others. For example, I post pictures on my weekly staff newsletter of teachers and students engaged in authentic literacy experiences, such as independent reading or shared writing. At the high school level, I regularly see leaders posting images with captions of their students' and teachers' successes on Twitter. Our aim is to direct our collective attention toward the actions that will lead to sustaining student achievement.

To ensure I am not favoring one person over another, I maintain a checklist of who I have recently recognized and have not. Along with our commitments and norms in place, recognizing everyone helps deter envious behavior.

Gratitude Project

Also referred to as a "holiday project," I send out a card with a picture of the staff member in action at school. The recipient is typically a staff member's parents, a sibling, or a friend. (No spouses, significant others, or children as they know how hard educators work.) Along with a picture is an inspiring message, such as, "May the joy they bring to our students be yours this holiday season."

This idea, suggested by former principal Whitaker (2012) at a school leadership conference, recognizes our staff member's commitment and efforts, and reminds our community of the same. Our work is made easier when we have the support of our families, community leaders, and school board.

Community Meals and Gifts

"Food symbolizes meals, and meals bring people together," notes literacy educator Judy Wallis (personal communication, August 13, 2021). "I never had a meeting without drinks and a snack (however meager). One of the things I know for sure is that it says, 'I knew you'd be here, and I planned for you.'" Meals can also be a regular event at your school and not cost a lot. For example, our staff sign up to bring in a dish for a monthly potluck lunch.

Even a simple treat may be all that is needed. Before staff meetings or professional development sessions, candies and healthy snacks are made available at the door and at tables. People come in, sit down, and commiserate while enjoying something to eat. In addition to food before meetings, gifts of thanks can also be effective for showing that we care. Practical items such as sticky notes, pens, journals, and books help make the faculty's work a little easier.

Reminding Teachers of Their Past Successes

Research has found that "people who experience small victories build the confidence—and the momentum—to keep going" (Wiest, 2018). In other words, past successes make it more likely someone will experience future success. We can show that we care by highlighting all the positive steps teachers have taken up to the present point. And the only way we know about their successes is if we are showing up regularly in classrooms with a nonjudgmental and supportive stance.

EXAMPLE 3.2: RECOGNIZING A TEACHER'S EFFORTS AND SUCCESSES

Jason stopped me after one of his lessons. "Can I run something by you?" I nodded. He directed me to the stacks of paper on his desk. Each stack offered a specific graphic organizer, such as a Venn diagram and the Frayer model. "I have shown my students how to use each one, using our current novel study to demonstrate it. I've invited students to pick one up as they read independently, but only a few have taken me up on this offer."

I paused and nodded, allowing us both to process the situation. Then I asked him if I could share a few observations. He accepted. "You seem a little frustrated with the progress so far." He agreed. I continued. "Let's consider all the efforts you have made and successes you have created so far. First, you took a bigger construct—nonlinguistic representations—and found a smaller, more manageable focus in graphic organizers. Second, you integrated this strategy into your current instruction independently. Third, you made these resources available to your kids and stated your belief that they can do it. Finally, I noticed that you have found a challenge in this process, and you are now thinking about how to improve. These are hallmarks of an effective teacher."

Jason raised his eyebrows and smiled, not having considered all the positive steps he had taken to get to this point. With his confidence intact, we transitioned to chatting about what he might do at this point.

CONDITION 3: COMMUNICATION

In Chapter 6, we take a deeper look at how to successfully communicate feedback that teachers can both accept and use. Feedback is a critical topic that deserves more attention as we lead more like a coach.

That said, communication has implications beyond coaching conversations. Strong communication skills help foster trust in the messenger as well as the message. We want to be perceived as *trustworthy* by all stakeholders, through what we say and how we present ourselves. In this section, I offer effective communication strategies for the five constituencies that leaders engage with: administrators (or like colleagues), teachers, students, parents, and the general public (Tschannen-Moran, 2014, p. 251). The key coaching skills and engaged listening are applicable within each context.

Communicating With Administrators/Peer Colleagues

Because we are on an "even playing field" with those who share similar positions to us, fostering trust with colleagues offers a unique challenge. For instance, we are sometimes vying for the same pool of resources that are always limited and often underfunded. These situations create conditions for conflict, which can be harmful to professional relationships.

Even with positionally alike colleagues, we can apply the previously mentioned coaching skills (paraphrase, pause, pose questions) during our conversations and interactions with colleagues.

For example, one question I find helpful when at an impasse with other administrators is to ask, "What are we *not* thinking of?" This is an invitation to explore new ideas and take up different perspectives. As a secondary administrator and athletic director, I would sometimes pose this inquiry to colleagues when trying to sort out academic schedules for shared faculty, or when assigning fields for a softball or baseball team when multiple games were planned. This question guides a group to consider what has not yet been considered.

Communicating With Teachers

When it comes to instructional leadership, our actions generally fall under two categories: support and challenge (Gabriel & Woulfin, 2017; Tschannen-Moran, 2014). Teachers want to know what the expectations are schoolwide (challenge), and they need resources, time, affirmation, and feedback to know they are progressing toward a goal or have achieved success (support). Having high expectations + high support conveys our faith in faculty members to achieve instructional excellence. We communicate this trust in ways beyond only our language: the environments we create and the behaviors we display.

Environments That Communicate Trust in Teachers

More than a simple open-door policy, leaders may want to rethink how their spaces are designed. For example, do visitors feel welcomed when they enter? What about the space helps teachers feel more at ease, and subsequently more likely to engage in coaching conversations? Next are a few ways I have set up my office to communicate my beliefs, confidence, and genuine appreciation for visitors.

Elements of My Office That Help Build Trust

- Diplomas and certificates of professional recognition hang prominently on my wall.
- A shelf holds professional books and resources I have read or plan to read.
- My desk faces the corner, so I can welcome a visitor without a physical barrier.
- Children's literature stands on another shelf, covers out.
- A circular table is in the middle of the room for meetings and group work.
- Personal artifacts, such as pictures of my family and fun trinkets, adorn my desk.
- A Star Wars poster hides behind my door (people appreciate knowing a fellow fan).

No one item says, "You can trust me." Yet each object says a little more about my life, as a person or as a professional. I want people to know me and what I am all about. At the very least, my environment gives us something small to talk about, which can help people relax.

Behaviors for Communicating Trust in Teachers

We build trust with teachers by our actions as much as by our words. In fact, our nonverbal communications, referred to as "paralanguage," can be more telling of our beliefs and our feelings about a situation (Costa et al., 2016).

The following behaviors can help communicate openness and presence.

Behaviors for Communicating Openness and Presence

❯ Direct eye contact (unless culturally frowned upon for one party)

❯ Nodding of head

❯ A respectful, nonjudgmental tone of voice

❯ Matching of the other person's pacing and volume during a coaching conversation without copying them (Costa et al., 2016, p. 43)

In addition, avoiding crossing our bodies with our arms or legs when facing another person can help remove visible barriers between each other. We appear more approachable and interested in what the other person is sharing. That is why I like round tables; we can sit more side-to-side with someone instead of communicating across a physical object.

These behaviors can all help in increasing trust and reducing anxiety or stress. Yet we might also acknowledge the "asymmetrical relationship" (Tschannen-Moran, 2014, p. 41) that exists between a leader and a teacher, especially when the leader is an administrator. "Because of the hierarchical nature of the relationships within a school, the principal exercises considerable authority over teachers and staff members" (Tschannen-Moran, 2014, pp. 40–41). This is the reality and still a necessary one to ensure schoolwide expectations are being met. However, the power that leaders hold (i.e., supervision, evaluation) can also inhibit productive conversations and professional growth. Is there a balance that can be struck?

A goal we might strive for in our communications as leaders is to be more vulnerable. Vulnerability is defined as "uncertainty, risk, and emotional exposure" (Brown, 2017, p. 154). One simple way is to request feedback from our staff about our performance. The very act of asking for this information shifts the perception of power, from leaders evaluating teachers to teachers critiquing leadership. In the past, I have set up a simple 1–4 rating scale with statements about different aspects of my practice. Teachers can respond anonymously so leaders get honest feedback. I have also noticed that through being vulnerable via surveys and other requests for feedback, more teachers become open to this approach for professional growth.

Another way we can display vulnerability is to apologize when we make mistakes. Tschannen-Moran (2014) suggests four steps for repairing trust between two people.

Repairing Trust

1. Admit it—acknowledge that the violation occurred

2. Apologize—to express regret

3. Ask for forgiveness

4. Amend your ways—commit to change (pp. 222-229)

As an example, the weekend before the 2020-2021 school year began, stress was high. Two teachers sent email messages to me revealing their anxiety. One was pointed. "I feel like we have not been adequately prepared for this school year. I am not feeling supported."

While reading, I felt negative emotions and thoughts rising to the surface. *Is it possible this year to feel adequately supported? This has never been done before!* Thankfully, I paused, took a breath, and responded to those concerned with the following:

> Thank you for reaching out to me. I am sorry you are not feeling supported at this time. I appreciate knowing how you feel. I wish I had more answers for you. For not providing more clarity, I apologize. If you want to talk through these challenges this weekend, please reach out to me at my home phone number. Really. I am here to support you.

The teachers responded back with appreciation. I did not get a call that weekend. Apparently, simply being available with a genuine invitation for assistance to amend the situation was what was needed.

WISDOM FROM THE FIELD: A DEFLATED BASKETBALL

Georgetown University men's basketball coach John Thompson kept a deflated basketball on his desk. His players remember the message he wanted to send them with this symbol. "Don't let the sum total of your existence be defined by 8 to 10 pounds of air," former player Joey Brown recalls him saying. "You're more than a basketball. Basketball is what you do. It's not who you are" (Walker, 2020).

What artifact, object, or symbol would be effective in communicating a big idea about your work? How might it make an impact on your faculty and staff? Jot down some ideas and thoughts in your journal.

Communicating With Students

Our impact on student achievement is largely indirect; we primarily influence teaching and learning through coaching conversations and other interactions with faculty members.

That said, there are opportunities for creating trusting environments and demonstrating trust-building behaviors for all members of a school, including students. Next are several actions leaders can take to convey faith and confidence in their capacity for success.

Leadership Actions for Communicating Trust in Students

- Invest significant funds in classrooms libraries, where students can freely check out texts to read independently.

- Encourage and promote student-led newsletters and digital communications about the activities occurring at school for a wide audience.

- Devote resources, space, and time for students to engage in self-directed learning projects, sometimes referred to as "Genius Hour" (Krebs & Zvi, 2020).

- As mentioned previously, make regular/daily appearances in classrooms for either brief informal visits or instructional walks.

- Read and respond to student writing or projects displayed around the school, celebrating these outcomes and their efforts.

- Be seen as a reader and writer, such as by carrying a book and/or a journal with you during classrooms visits.

One example is in my city's own high school. Students create daily video messages for their classmates and the community. They communicate recent events, celebrate their peers, and provide information about future opportunities. School leaders, both administration and teachers, secured one room for this purpose. A green screen plus audio and video recording technologies were provided. Their digital media announcements are posted online so anyone can watch and comment. What is typically managed by the adults—morning announcements—is now entrusted to the students. Also worth noting is the modeling for teachers of what's possible for instruction with these types of activities.

Communicating With Families

Our level of trust in our students is intertwined with the trust we have in their families. Studies have found that educators tend to associate a student's performance at school with what they perceive in their family's ability to parent (Tschannen-Moran, 2014, p. 189).

This sense of trust is developed not just in our academic expectations. We can also communicate that we care. Kind notes about their child sent home, sharing photos depicting a positive classroom community, and making phone calls when concerned about a student's experience at school all support the development of trust between home and school. These are expectations of families as well as educators. As one parent described it succinctly to me, "All I want is for my daughter to get smarter and to be cared for."

When concerns are raised, we do well to lead like a coach in these situations. This includes utilizing the three key coaching skills when interacting with a family member and leveraging instructional walks as a source of knowledge about the classroom.

For example, in a previous school a parent expressed concerns about their child not being challenged enough in mathematics. "He understands and is ready for something more challenging while most of the class is still learning the concept being taught." As the parent spoke over the phone, I gave them ample time to talk by pausing, along with letting them know I was hearing what they were saying through paraphrasing. ("You have concerns that your child is not being challenged enough.")

Sensing that they wanted to say something but unsure about how to go about it, I asked if I could pose a question; she agreed. "I am hearing several concerns about the classroom in general, beyond only differentiation in mathematics. Are you looking for a more significant change in your son's education?" Through this informed question, made possible by engaged listening, I learned that a new classroom placement was the larger goal. At that point, I was able to explain our school practices and how we rarely move kids midyear.

This situation was not resolved that day; the parent continued to assert their desire to move their child. But by continuing to engage with the family so they felt understood as well as heard, and by relying on my knowledge gained from my regular instructional walks, we had developed a better sense of trust between home and school. The parent did eventually come to accept their child's placement, and even became more of a partner with the teacher in advocating for their child more appropriately.

Communicating With the General Public

Unlike other constituencies, our relationship with the public is mediated largely by third parties, such as the media and newsletters. Even without a direct link, these relationships are important. Many community members have extended family in the local educational system. They vote on referendums for additional school funding. All staff need to take responsibility for building trust with the larger community if we want their support.

Messaging is a key strategy. Memorable phrases, attractive visuals, and readable content for online and in-print publications can be used to garner support and keep the public informed. Messages can go anywhere. In my previous school, we purchased T-shirts with our name and mascot printed for our students and staff once a year. "Proud to be a Bulldog!" was observed often in the neighborhood. We were proud of our school, and we wanted our community to join us in that sense of belonging.

Writing articles for the local newspaper can highlight specific issues. Getting ahead of the conversation and helping the public understand how a decision directly affects one's school helps people understand what is at stake. Our goal is to guide readers to connect the dots versus telling them what to think. It is more respectful and less preachy. (See *Writing to Persuade: How to Bring People Over to Your Side,* 2019, by Trish Hall, former editor of the *New York Times* Op-Ed page, for a guide on how to craft articles that influence others.)

One-on-one correspondence may be the most effective form of communication. You have your audience's complete attention. This can be in person, over the phone, or a personal email. However we choose to communicate with the public, it is important that we always maintain a respectful tone and approach.

This is where our coaching skills can also be beneficial. Pausing, paraphrasing, and posing questions all work effectively for engaged listening when communicating with the public. We do not have to agree with what a misinformed individual proclaims. If a situation becomes heated, phrases such as, "I appreciate knowing where you stand on this issue," or "Can I get back to you on this later?" can help diffuse a situation.

While it is said that we cannot overcommunicate, we can improve our messaging by differentiating how we communicate with all stakeholders.

Online newsletters and school blogs can be a powerful way of letting teachers, students, families, and the community know about what is happening in our schools. Families and community members can see what teachers and students are currently learning. Teachers and students can learn what their colleagues and peers are up to as well.

I have found the following types of content to be most conducive for newsletters or blogs:

- An image from a classroom that celebrates the learning process
- A personal story or example that relates to a bigger idea about education
- General updates of recent events and what is coming up
- Recommended content, such as a professional article, educational video, or podcast

A blog or a newsletter can communicate the positive aspects of our current reality and a vision of where we want to be schoolwide. Subsequently, these visible recognitions build trust in our capacity for success, which leads to confidence in our future endeavors.

EXAMPLE 3.3: CO-CREATING A PLAN FOR SELF-DIRECTED LEARNERS

I paraphrased what we knew at this moment. "You located the graphic organizers next to your desk after modeling each one with a book you are all reading together." After a pause, Jason asked, "Do you think the location of the graphic organizers is what is preventing students from wanting to use them? Maybe they feel self-conscious about going up to my desk to grab one in front of their peers."

We agreed that 14- and 15-year-olds care a lot about peers' perceptions of them. "Okay . . . where else could we place them?" As we scanned the room, Jason noted a metal filing cabinet in a back corner of the room. At the time it held assignments from previous lessons that students could take if they were absent, or if their work was missing. "It seems worth trying," I acknowledged. Jason transferred the graphic organizers to that location.

Before his next class came in, I asked him what data he would collect to know whether students were utilizing this tool for their learning. "Well, I could count how many sheets there are for each graphic organizer now, and then see what's left after a week." I congratulated him on finding a quantitative way of measuring his students' response to this instructional strategy. We agreed to meet next week to analyze the results.

CONDITION 4: COMPETENCE

Think about the last business you went to for groceries, home supplies, or a gift for someone. Why did you go there? We rarely think about these choices, but the likely reason is you trust their business to provide a quality product or service at a fair price. Your trust is supported by your confidence in their capacity to meet your needs.

This is competence. It goes beyond mere consistency; it is being perceived as able to produce regular results. Competence can be augmented with compassion, such as offering to take your groceries to the car. Communication through advertising and messaging can remind us about a business's ability to deliver on the goods or services promised. But the three previous elements of trust ring hollow if promises and responsibilities are not fulfilled.

In the context of supporting teaching and learning, competence becomes more complex both in how leaders achieve results and in how they are perceived by others through this lens. In any school, you may find a teacher or two wanting to be directed on what to teach, how to teach, and when. A few others prefer complete autonomy, to be able to shut their door and do their work. The majority want both direction for a schoolwide goal and some authority to make decisions on behalf of their students. These varied agendas can complicate our capacity to lead and decrease our own sense of competence and confidence.

Facilitating schoolwide dialogue can help us understand where people are at on an issue. The idea is to create a safe space using routines to surface people's concerns, questions, and suggestions. These routines, such as the protocols found at the School Reform Initiative (www.schoolreforminitiative.org), provide structure to glean insights into how the faculty feel about and view the current school climate. The leader, in response, can use this information to systematically address issues either on their own or with teams. We build trust by doing what we will say we will do, as well as working together to accomplish these tasks. As Tschannen-Moran (2014) notes, "pursuing small, early wins on some key tasks can help build trust in both the principal's and the school's competence" (p. 257).

One example is when I first came to my current school, in Mineral Point, Wisconsin. My superintendent at the time, Luke Francois (personal communication, August 17, 2016), recommended that I start my tenure by listening to the staff and offering support for addressing issues. He suggested the idea of an open suitcase at a staff meeting. Staff could write down their anonymous concerns on slips of paper, fold them up, and then put them in the suitcase. Once ready, I closed the suitcase in front of them and announced,

> Thank you for sharing these with me. I plan to read each one, as well as to organize these concerns and suggestions around central issues I can address now and in the future. Also, please note that now that you have shared these with me, you no longer need to worry about them so much.

The concerns were specific and helpful in understanding the current school situation. Next are a few of their comments in Table 3.1, under five different themes that I ascertained in the review.

For the rest of that first school year and beyond, I created a list around these concerns. I would work toward addressing one issue, find a way

Table 3.1 Staff feedback from suitcase activity

Staff trust in each other	Staff trust in administrators	Too many initiatives, not enough time	Curriculum and instructional coherence	Professional expectations and consistency
"When things aren't accepted or when we don't get our way, we are unable to move on."	"Don't micromanage!"	"Keep family first. In the past, we were given lots of 'things' to do."	"It would be beneficial for students and staff if we all agreed on the reading curriculum.	"Not all staff are listened to and treated the same."

to make the results visible, and then share these results publicly as a schoolwide celebration such as in my newsletter.

Instructional walks also develop a perception of competence. Teachers participate in dialogue around our practice and feel like the professionals they are. We learn from each other, see past our singular roles of teacher or leader, and engage in continuous learning, which leads to an increase in trust in others and confidence in ourselves.

EXAMPLE 3.4: ANALYZING OUR RESULTS, FOLLOWING THE INQUIRY

Jason was excited to share the results of his decision to move the graphic organizers to a more neutral area of the classroom. He handed me a handwritten table that tallied how many sheets were used by his students in one week's time (Table 3.2).

Table 3.2 Table of graphic organizer usage

Graphic organizer	Number of sheets used	Context notes
Venn diagram	16	It is a tool that other teachers in the school have used with the students.
Frayer model	5	It was only modeled once and briefly for the students.
Concept map	2	Concepts and themes are challenging for students to use without lots of modeling and support.

After I read his results and notes, I congratulated him. "This is great data to have for your practice. What are your initial impressions?"

"It seems like the more the students are exposed to a tool, especially when it is modeled by the teacher, the more likely they are to use it." I nodded, paused, then followed up with, "Anything else?"

"Well, I am curious as to how other teachers are applying the strategy of nonlinguistic representation, and not just graphic organizers." Internally, I could feel the excitement of facilitating peer observations bubbling up, but I paused and then calmly suggested a few teachers who he might want to observe. It helped that I had visited these faculty members as well, frequently and informally.

(Continued)

(Continued)

Summarizing the Experience

I want to point out a few aspects of this experience that connect the dots regarding leading like a coach.

First, I leaned on specific coaching skills—paraphrasing, posing questions, pausing—when partnering with Jason in this professional learning. I suppressed any agenda I might have or suggestions to try. Second and related, I remained open and ready to learn with Jason. Creating this space for collaboration was aligned with a collective commitment in my school. These two aspects are visually summarized in Figure 3.2.

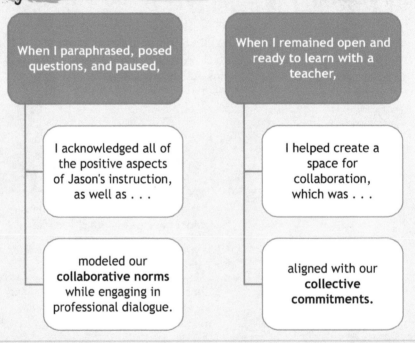

Figure 3.2 Collaborative norms and collective commitments

When I paraphrased, posed questions, and paused,

When I remained open and ready to learn with a teacher,

I acknowledged all of the positive aspects of Jason's instruction, as well as . . .

I helped create a space for collaboration, which was . . .

modeled our **collaborative norms** while engaging in professional dialogue.

aligned with our **collective commitments.**

Finally, this experience would likely not have gone as well as it did without the four elements of trust providing the foundation for my first forays into leading like a coach.

- I was *consistent* in my presence, showing up and deferring to his learning goals.

- I demonstrated *compassion* when he was frustrated with initial results—for example, highlighting all the successes he had achieved so far.

- I *communicated* my belief that he could engage in professional inquiry.

- Jason's initial results helped him develop a higher level of *competence* in this instructional strategy.

- The ultimate result was a *sense of confidence*, displayed in his curiosity and in his courage to observe his colleagues also applying these strategies.

TEACH IN THE CLASSROOM

Sometimes teachers need to see an instructional strategy or practice in action, often more than once. A critical element of competence is credibility. Can we engage in the very actions we are asking teachers to employ in the classrooms successfully? Teachers' respect in our capacity to lead increases when they see us "walk the walk."

That is why I advocate for school leaders to get into classrooms and teach. If the lesson goes well, we have successfully demonstrated that an instructional approach is valid and could be implemented. If the lesson does not go as well as planned, it is an opportunity to be vulnerable and prone to error. We humanize ourselves and we give permission to the teachers to make mistakes without recourse.

These lessons do not have to be elaborate projects or multiple-day sessions. In fact, the simpler the better. Next are some initial ideas for getting into the classroom.

- *Read aloud to students:* This is an acceptable practice in any grade level, all the way up through high school. Read the book ahead of time to ensure content and language are appropriate. Offer this within the context of getting to know the students. Next are some of my favorite texts for reading aloud.

  - Elementary School Level: *Last Stop on Market Street* by Matt de la Peña; *Meet the Dogs of Bedlam Farm* by Jon Katz

  - Middle School Level: *The Wretched Stone* by Chris Van Allsberg; *Hear My Voice: The Testimonies of Children Detained at the Southern Border of the United States* by Warren Binford (and several authors and illustrators)

  - High School Level: *Poetry 180: A Turning Back to Poetry* by Billy Collins (and other poets); *The Moth Presents* series by Catherine Burns (several writers)

- *Cover a teacher's classroom:* Teachers sometimes need staff to step in and take over instruction to attend an IEP (Individualized Educational Program) meeting or a special event. Leading instruction in these situations can build trust and confidence on two levels: it shows we care about their other responsibilities, and we present ourselves as competent educators.

- *Lead special schoolwide events:* Like filling in for a teacher, leading a schoolwide event positions you as a trusted educator in the eyes of others. For example, in recent winter months we have hosted online community read-ins. From the warmth of our homes, staff and myself read aloud selected picture books to students in the evening, using video conferencing tools. The families have a copy of the book so they can follow along and reread later.

CONCLUSION: TRUST STARTS WITH US

For trust to be fostered and sustained in a school, it starts with us as leaders. Whether it is extending opportunities for professionals to learn or to be the recipients of these invitations, it begins by seeing others as capable and having good intentions. We believe they are competent individuals who are compassionate toward students and colleagues, consistent in their actions, and can communicate effectively with others.

And if that is not the case, then it is up to us to both demonstrate and expect these qualities in the school. This is where leading like a coach begins: Are we fully listening to what the other person is saying? Do they feel heard? When I visit classrooms, is my intent to first understand and appreciate teachers' and students' efforts? How will I let them know this? We cannot wait for others to set the tone and form the rules for how people operate within a school. Our positional power is best utilized when teachers understand that leadership is not just a position but also a way of being, that they have power too.

These efforts point toward a fifth "C": *collaboration*—moving forward together, with agreement on the focus. This is the aim for the next chapter: organizing around a priority.

SUCCESS INDICATORS FOR CREATING CONFIDENCE THROUGH TRUST

- The staff start coming to you directly with their concerns versus only their colleagues. This shows they trust you with the information they are sharing and believe you can help resolve the situation if not solve it. To sustain trust, ask them what they want from you when they come to you with a concern: to coach, to collaborate, or to consult (Lipton & Wellman, 2007). In my experience, much of the time staff simply want you to listen.

- Administer a specific survey with staff about their trust in you as a leader. For a tool to tease out areas of strength and growth, check out the nine questions developed by Bryk and Schneider (2002) in *Trust in Schools: A Core Resource for Improvement*. This information will give you feedback on how you can grow as a leader regarding trust, plus model vulnerability with your faculty.

- Visitors will describe your school in positive ways. "This is such as a welcoming school" and "Everyone seems happy here" are possible comments you may hear from the public. People are noticing the verbal and nonverbal ways the staff and students interact with each other. To reinforce this trusting environment, document these positive comments digitally and share out this list of affirmations with staff from time to time. The more we view how others perceive us, the more we believe it and come to identify with these perceptions.

 # Reflective Questions

Consider the following questions to promote reflection. You can respond to them in writing and/or in conversation with colleagues.

1. What are three key takeaways for you after reading this chapter?

2. Of the four elements of trust, which two do you believe are currently strengths within your practice? What evidence supports this belief?

3. Of the four elements of trust, which one would you like to improve in? What specific actions can you take to grow in this area?

ORGANIZE AROUND A PRIORITY

4

> *When teams can focus on the purpose of the work and identify what is noise and what are data, they lay the foundation for decisions that are manageable and that feel safe enough to try.*

—Kim and Gonzales-Black (2018, p. 109)

If you knew that your last day at your school was tomorrow, how would you decide to spend your time? For me, I would not be checking email, entering requisitions, or signing reports. Instead, you would find me in classrooms and in common areas, connecting with students, staff, and parents.

If you knew that your last day at your school was tomorrow, how would you decide to spend your time?

Why wait until the last day? Why not make our every-day actions reflect our values as school leaders? How we choose to engage in our school each day communicates our beliefs as educators. It means organizing ourselves and our school around a priority.

Merriam-Webster (n.d.-b) defines "priority" as "something given or meriting attention before competing alternatives." Our priority is the first thing we typically do or plan for, the experience we initially schedule into our days. This is why when I add events to my calendar, I first set aside time in classrooms.

Trust serves as a foundation for being able to collaboratively move toward a vision of student success. It underpins the necessary conversations among faculty members to create clarity around the goal. For example, the professional inquiry with Jason was mediated by our school's focus while supported by our efforts to build trust. These efforts create confidence not only in one's practice but also in the journey itself (Figure 4.1). Teachers need to believe that the professional learning journey they are taking will be a fruitful one for their students and themselves.

A point of clarification: A goal is not the priority. A goal is more tangible. For example, students becoming better readers is a priority. A goal would exist within that priority, such as implementing comprehension strategies or building students' love for reading. These goals are aligned with a priority and can be assessed to measure progress. The priority is broad; a goal is specific.

The rest of this chapter describes the steps for organizing a school's attention, efforts, and resources around a priority.

Figure 4.1 Trust supporting a schoolwide priority

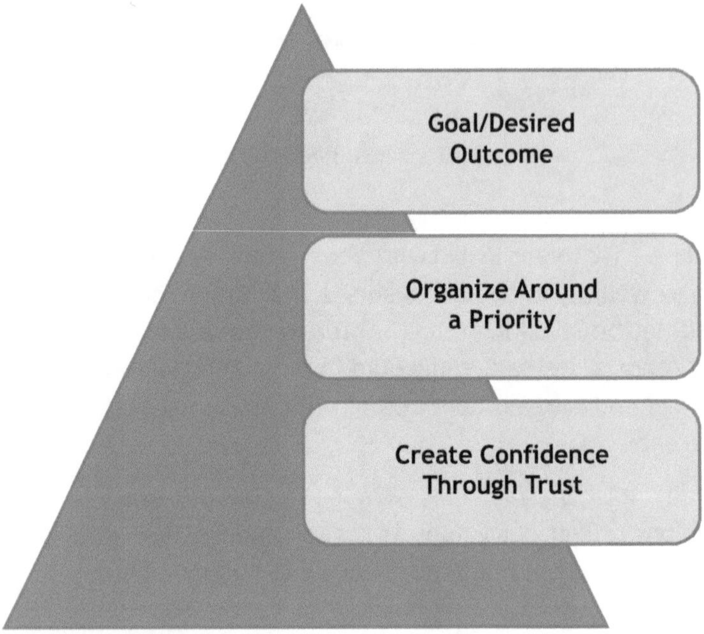

Goal/Desired
Outcome

Organize Around
a Priority

Create Confidence
Through Trust

STEPS FOR ORGANIZING AROUND A PRIORITY

Step 1: Analyze and understand your current reality

Step 2: Examine your beliefs about instruction

Step 3: Engage in focused professional learning

Step 4: Create collective commitments around promising practices

At every step, leading like a coach is the primary stance when working with faculty and students in continuous improvement. We do more listening than talking when attempting to understand our status as a school. We let our current beliefs determine our starting point instead of relying solely on test scores. We all engage in professional learning that is meaningful to our practice versus only getting trained in the latest commercial resource. And we develop specific commitments about what works for our students, so we have a common language for effectively engaging in professional collaboration. The only way we achieve success is together. There is no going it alone on these initiatives.

STEP 1: ANALYZE AND UNDERSTAND YOUR CURRENT REALITY

Just as we do not want our schools to be judged by a single test score, or our evaluations to be based on a handful of random observations, we also do not want our schoolwide focus to be driven by a single data point. We need a 360-degree view to have a more accurate picture of our learning community. A broader perspective requires multiple data points to develop a better understanding of our current reality.

A framework for continuous school improvement, introduced by Bernhardt (2015), starts off with a series of questions to guide this data analysis:

- Where are we now?

- How did we get here?

- Where do we want to be?

- How are we going to get there?

- Is what we are doing making a difference?

These questions are challenging to answer in isolation. That is why leaders need to develop an instructional leadership team (Routman, 2014). This team, made up of current faculty members, is tasked with making professional learning decisions on behalf of the school. A critical step in developing this team is *conducting interviews with interested teachers*. Having faculty serve as leaders not only helps with empowering our staff but also gives teachers the opportunity to develop their leadership skills for the future.

The Instructional Leadership Team Selection Process

To begin, I send out a role description and overall purpose to all staff. In addition, I include questions I will ask them during the interview. These questions are based on a relevant article that highlights promising practices. (A favorite article is from *Educational Leadership*, "Every Child, Every Day" by Richard Allington and Rachael Gabriel (2012). Secondary leaders may find Chaunté Garrett's (2021) article "Relevant Curriculum is Equitable Curriculum" from the same journal helpful for this purpose.) The interview process and the article help filter those unwilling to adopt a broader perspective on behalf of the school and all students.

Teachers set up an appointment to interview with me. I do reach out to a few key teachers in the building and encourage them to apply for the team. They are individuals who have shown promise as teacher-leaders in their instruction, their positivity, and their ability to take others' perspectives.

During the interview, I am an engaged listener, like our conversations at the end of an instructional walk. Technology is put away. While the experience resembles a formal interview, our time together usually became more of a conversation. Here is an example:

Me: What was surprising to you after reading the article?

Teacher: Well, I found myself realizing that we don't have students writing every day in our classrooms, as the authors recommend.

Me: I have noticed that in other classrooms, too. As a potential member of our instructional leadership team, how do you think we might respond?

Teacher: (*brief silence for her to think*) Maybe we could look at our school schedule and identify ways to better incorporate writing into the literacy block. We could also integrate writing in the content areas.

Me: I appreciate these ideas. They do not involve adding on to the day, but rather rethinking how we use our time. Let's make sure they become a part of a future conversation with the leadership team.

Every teacher who has ever interviewed with me has been accepted. (I let them know right after the interview is complete that they are "in.")

We attract the right candidates because our intentions are made clear about the type of members we are looking for. If a candidate is not a good fit, offer to explain why when letting them know they were not accepted—an opportunity to coach. If they decline the feedback, that may be confirmation that they are not a good fit at this time.

We culminate the process with a celebration at the next staff meeting. New leadership team members are introduced to the rest of the faculty. This time is also used to remind everyone that this team is a decision-making body. While we will be visible in our work, such as sharing out agendas and opening meetings up for anyone to attend and listen, our group had the authority to determine our professional learning activities on behalf of staff, students, and the larger community. This transparency helps ensure that future decisions made will be met with less resistance.

The process of interviewing teachers for an instructional leadership team has many benefits.

Benefits of Interviews for Instructional Leadership Team

- I can work smarter as a school leader. I do not have to be the source of all ideas.

- It professionalizes a sometimes-arbitrary committee and gives the team a larger and more important purpose.

- By sharing the roles and resources that would guide our work, the entire staff is aware of our schoolwide focus and the direction we would be heading in the future.

Once the instructional leadership team is formed, a first agenda item can be developing a decision-making matrix. Clarifying what it is the school will focus on and how it is determined forces everyone to make a commitment to what matters most right now. It also ensures that teacher-leaders understand what their role is during leadership conversations.

Routman (2012) suggests breaking down the decision-making process into three areas: (1) by consensus, (2) by majority vote, and/or (3) by the principal.

Here is a start to the development of a decision-making matrix within each area.

Decisions made by consensus	Decisions made by majority vote	Decisions made by the principal
Professional development focus, activities, and schedule	Acquisition of a new curriculum resource	Final selection for hiring a new teacher

You will notice that all these examples have an impact on schoolwide instruction. It is important to convey to faculty that the role of the instructional leadership team is focusing on teaching and learning, and how to continuously improve. Nonacademic decisions can be made outside the purview of this team, such as with a separate committee. Leadership team members appreciate the respect for their time and knowing that their insights make a positive difference on behalf of the school.

ACTIVITY 4.1 — DEVELOP A DECISION-MAKING MATRIX

Think about the current priorities at your school. Add the decisions you are working on this year into the appropriate section of this matrix. Revisit this process annually to review and revise as needed.

Decisions made by consensus	Decisions made by majority vote	Decisions made by the principal

The Data Analysis Process

To develop a comprehensive view of our school's current reality, we often do not need more data. We need different data. Multiple perspectives help us better understand what is going well and what needs improvement. In addition, there needs to be an effective process in place to analyze the data and arrive at an accurate conclusion.

Bernhardt (2015) recommends that leaders organize data into four categories:

1. Demographics (attendance, behavior referrals, percentage of students living in poverty)

2. Processes (curriculum management, professional learning, program offerings)

3. Perceptions (school climate, schoolwide expectations, student/teacher attitudes)

4. Student learning (benchmark assessments/screeners, teachers' written observations, test scores)

A leadership team can then go through each data set and start developing theories about what is leading to these results.

What multiple categories of data provide goes beyond only focusing on test scores to drive future professional learning. It helps support or contradict any theory proposed. For example, one school's initial theory was they needed to focus on math instruction; their standardized assessment results in that area were low (Kim & Gonzales-Black, 2018). Yet when they dug into the different data sets, including their curriculum management processes, they discovered that the more likely reason for low schoolwide proficiency in mathematics was that the students had trouble reading the math textbook. The text complexity was too high for some kids. They had examined many sides of the problem and found a more probable conclusion. This realization led to an increased effort in learning about and implementing more effective reading instruction in the content areas.

In my current school, we made somewhat similar conclusions in literacy. We examined different sets of data and developing a better understanding of the challenge. Our leadership team collected and presented data in the different areas to understand our current reality around a driving question. Figure 4.2 highlights a few of our findings.

Figure 4.2 Data analysis in the four categories

Driving question: Are our students succeeding as readers and writers?

Demographics	**Processes**
- 11% of our students have an IEP - 30% of our students experience financial hardship	- Wednesday afternoons devoted to professional learning communities - No common routines for examining beliefs, instructional strategies, or classroom resources

Data Findings

Perceptions	**Student Learning**
- Feedback from families are positive about the school - Trust is a challenge, with leadership and among faculty	- We exceed expectations (state report card) - Student growth in reading is below the state average

Looking at these conclusions, we decided to engage in a whole-school professional study around the foundations of literacy. This study took place once a month during our weekly professional learning community time.

SPECIAL NOTE: WHEN TO BRING IN AN EDUCATIONAL CONSULTANT

Data analysis and knowing what to do with that information is difficult work. An outside perspective in the form of an educational consultant can be helpful to leaders in making sense of student assessment results.

In addition, an educational consultant can serve as an external facilitator for professional discussion and learning. Change can be challenging for a few teachers to accept. They may openly resist professional learning around a priority. A consultant can help you say what needs to be said.

For example, when Routman (2014) was in the second year of working with a school focused on writing instruction, one resistant teacher asked her what she might do to improve. Regie responded by reminding her of all the support she had received over the past two years from the building leaders. "Now it's your turn to do the hard work required to become an excellent writing teacher" (p. 23).

STEP 2: EXAMINE YOUR BELIEFS ABOUT INSTRUCTION

Our profession struggles to create clarity around what is effective instruction. It is partly due to the complex nature of education.

For example, we have had debates for decades on the best way to teach readers. We look for "proof" that a certain practice or resource or strategy is a best practice.

What we find is context matters regarding our implementation of any instructional approach. Every year teachers receive a new group of students with varying levels of background knowledge and prior skills. We need to both keep up with current research and respond to our kids' needs.

Therefore, educators can first examine their beliefs about instruction as they organize around a priority. Awareness around the focus for the organization is the *what*. Everyone understands the priority and has input in developing it so they can support it, and actively work toward implementing whatever practice the school deems effective. But teachers also want to know the *why*. It goes beyond only data or research supporting a practice. When teachers believe in the work at a deep and personal level, they are more willing to commit to it over the long term.

To increase faculty commitment and raise expectations for an improved educational experience, schools can first create awareness around our actions in classrooms and then examine the beliefs that lead to improvement schoolwide.

1. Create awareness around our actions in the classroom.

Beyond building trust, creating awareness is my initial purpose when conducting instructional walks. I want to be a mirror for teachers' practice. Yes, it is important to acknowledge what they are doing well, but it is also important to notice everything in the classroom. What are students and faculty saying? What are they doing? What is the environment like? Think of yourself as a newspaper reporter, opening with a story about the learning experience in each classroom—just the facts.

For example, as I engaged in instructional walks one year, I could see the influence of our school's new library media technology specialist. Book sets checked out from the library were displayed in reading centers. Students were utilizing new technologies during the literacy block that had been previously modeled by our librarian. Yet this was only observed in some classrooms. *How can I help all faculty members see the services our library provides as part of their literacy curriculum?* I wondered.

2. Examine our beliefs about students and our practices.

Broadening one's knowledge base does not mean someone will change their beliefs about a practice. People may say one thing but will act in contradiction to their words. Examining beliefs helps us discover (a) why we hold them, (b) if there are any potential problems with our current beliefs, (c) what is preventing us from rethinking them, and (d) what reasonable steps we might take to better understand the impact of our beliefs on student learning.

One approach to examining schoolwide beliefs is responding to a list of statements related to the priority. In my case, we wanted to improve our literacy instruction. So we read through over 20 statements developed by Regie Routman about foundational literacy instruction. Teachers responded anonymously with either "true" or "false" to each one. Some statements are aligned with effective instruction, some are not, and some are ambiguous and invite discussion. Next are two examples:

- ▶ Elementary Example: "You can teach phonics and skills with a child's written story and assess their phonemic awareness by examining their journal writing."

- ▶ Secondary Example: "Students who use graphic organizers while reading have better comprehension."

(For more information on developing beliefs statements around literacy, check out Regie's website at regieroutman.org.)

Examining schoolwide beliefs can take place within one staff meeting. Statements are posed in a digital form to get immediate results. Once everyone has responded, we celebrate any belief statements that we agree on unanimously. In my experience, if trust has been developed at least initially, schools will find agreement around at least two or three statements. Figure 4.3 highlights a few beliefs with which my current school found agreement.

A local graphic designer, Kristin Mitchell, developed this visual once we found agreement on the statements. They are printed on posters to display in classrooms and on notebooks that are handed out during professional learning experiences. These tangible wins bring a faculty closer together. As Kim and Gonzales-Black (2018) note, "There is no more important trust-building activity than achieving success together" (p. 54).

Figure 4.3 Shared beliefs

Our Beliefs About the Reading–Writing Connection

1. You can teach phonics and skills with a child's written story and assess their phonemic awareness by examining their journal writing.

2. Shared writing that evolves from common experiences are often the easiest texts to read and is an excellent way to connect to reading.

3. Young children do not need to know all their letters and sounds before they can write stories and read back their writing.

4. Explaining vocabulary through interactive read-aloud can lead to students applying that vocabulary in their reading and writing.

5. Reading excellent literature and/or hearing quality literature read aloud positively influences students' writing quality.

6. For struggling readers, reading their own writing is often their first successful reading experience.

The next step in the examination of our collective beliefs is a faculty discussion in why we did or did not find agreement. This is our opportunity to clarify our understanding about instruction and start the process of organizing around our priority with specific practices. Questions that can help the discussion include the following:

▶ Why do we believe _____ (a specific practice from one belief statement) is effective for all our students?

▶ Are there any potential problems with _____ (a belief the school now owns)?

▶ What prevented us from adopting _____ (a belief where there was a small percentage of faculty not agreeing to it)?

▶ What reasonable steps might we take to embed these beliefs schoolwide?

To be fair, beliefs can be a double-edged sword. While they guide our actions toward implementing promising literacy strategies, they can also leave us stuck in outdated practices if we are not willing to continuously reexamine our current practices. It is a paradox; we commit to our beliefs while remaining open to new ideas.

Yet we must find a focus and organize our efforts around this priority. My predecessor at my previous school had a saying: "You've got to believe it to achieve it." To really believe in something means it becomes a part of our practice. We grow in our profession only when we become more critical about our currently held beliefs and regularly examine them through reading professionally, intentional reflection, and action. Education is constantly evolving, considering new studies and findings. To stay current, a mindset open to options seems necessary.

STEP 3: ENGAGE IN FOCUSED PROFESSIONAL LEARNING

Ian Jukes, an educational thought leader, ran a blog titled "The Committed Sardine." He used the analogy of a school of sardines to describe how organizations changed direction toward a new goal:

> 100 percent of the sardines do not turn in the new direction at the same time. Only a small number of sardines, 10-15 percent, committed to leading the change cause the entire mass to move in the new direction. Once the few make the turn, the rest of the school follow. (W. Hall, 2012)

This metaphor serves as an example for how we might lead professional change. The goal is not to convince everyone right away of the new approach to teaching and learning. Instead, we can make the case for the new direction, provide opportunities to try it and apply it, and then translate these attempts into quick wins in the classroom with the help of instructional walks. Once some teachers see the results and speak positively about the experience, others are more likely to adopt the ideas and trust the process.

1. Make the case for the new direction.

To persuade others, we can approach faculty in multiple ways. There needs to be some logic and research to support the initiative. Yet people are not persuaded by data alone. They also need to be personally invested in the change emotionally. As a wise person once shared, "The distance between knowing and doing is feeling."

In my example with the reading-writing connection, we started with classroom libraries. We studied Regie Routman's resources, including articles and videos of teachers leading students in the co-organization of the texts. I also highlighted recent research that supports more than only putting books into a classroom. For example, Yi et al. (2019) found that while bringing in texts into a classroom can have benefits, such as students checking more books out and reading outside the school day, access to texts alone was not enough. A few conclusions:

- No increase in authentic instruction during independent reading time

- No expectations for reading independently

- No effect on student reading achievement

"In other words," I shared at one professional learning session, "simply putting books in a classroom may not lead to better readers."

We combined the examples and study with personal stories. I spoke about how I became an engaged reader when my third-grade teacher read aloud books to us from her classroom library.

At this point, teachers were invited to write or share their own personal experiences with colleagues on how they became engaged readers and the role school played in their lives. By guiding the faculty to remember their own journey with learning, initiated with both logic and narrative, teachers are more likely to embrace a new approach to instruction.

2. Provide opportunities to try it and apply it.

We do not change behaviors by talking about it or making a strong case for the initiative. Professionals need to physically engage in the change and experience it for the process of instructional improvement to occur.

Think about anything you have become proficient at, if not an expert in. Gardening, cooking/baking, or playing guitar all rely on lots of opportunities to practice with the actual tools of the trade. If we are lucky to have a guide on the side, their support and feedback accelerate the learning process. Even if we are learning on our own, the large number of resources available online and in print can help us improve in any area.

In our school's first attempts with involving students in organizing the classroom library, they already had this initial support in the videos, articles, and professional discussions. What we also needed were more books and furniture for housing these texts. So we dedicated a portion of our Title I budget to making these purchases over the summer.

Teachers were then given a month, at the beginning of the school year, to co-organize the classroom libraries with students and use them as part of authentic literacy instruction. Reminders were sent out about why we were doing this and the potential impact it could have on student literacy engagement and achievement. My role as school leader was to be in classrooms as this process occurred to support their attempts via instructional walks.

3. Translate instructional attempts into quick wins.

In the initial stages of schoolwide improvement, the initial goal is not to change people's minds. It is to create opportunities for success. We can foster the conditions for quick wins by noticing and naming their efforts using the language of the practice, as well as explicitly describing how their actions contribute to student learning.

In our initial attempts with classroom libraries, I wrote down the process in action during instructional walks:

▶ Teacher and student dialogue

▶ Description of the environment and the actions

▶ Articulation of the general feeling of the experience

In many of the classrooms, I was also able to take pictures of everyone's efforts (Figure 4.4). For some images I would use a digital

Figure 4.4 Elementary classroom library

application and add an annotation with my positive observations. These images would be presented as a slide show at the next staff meeting.

Promising classroom libraries for older students may have more complex texts, but they share the common thread of student ownership—for example, through selection of which books to display and to recommend to peers (Figures 4.5 and 4.6).

Important to note is I did not differentiate between levels of implementation, such as teachers co-organizing their entire classroom library or only one section. Also, I celebrated every classroom to ensure that there was equity in my recognition and accountability in our efforts. The message is clear: everyone needs to engage in this process for all kids to have access to an excellent education.

For resistant staff, Kim and Gonzales-Black (2018) recommend asking, "What is safe enough to try?" (p. 100). It gives teachers an entry point

Figure 4.5 Middle grades classroom library

Figure 4.6 High school classroom library

into the process by making first attempts small and manageable. There is little risk if things do not go as expected.

During instructional walks, I describe the action and the effect of teachers' decision-making: what they did and how it affected their students in a positive way. This recognition helps ensure these actions become habits in every classroom if they are not already. Associating this affirmation with an image creates a sense of clarity about what we are aiming for as a school that cannot be matched.

ACTIVITY 4.2 DIFFERENTIATE YOUR RECOGNITION OF EFFECTIVE INSTRUCTION

During your next instructional walk, take a picture of instruction in action and share the images with teachers. Add a comment about why you think the images show effective instruction.

STEP 4: CREATE COLLECTIVE COMMITMENTS AROUND PROMISING PRACTICES

Two years after we engaged in professional learning around co-organizing classroom libraries, I visited a classroom for my first instructional walk of the year. Right away, I could tell the teacher had not included students in the process. It had all the telltale signs:

- Pinterest-perfect labels on the book bins
- Colored stickers on the spines to denote genre
- Not a book out of place

I was feeling my frustration surface. Yet I went about my purpose, writing down what was going well and posing questions for the teacher.

After handing the teacher my notes, which documented the joyful experience during the read-aloud (*Because of Winn-Dixie* by Kate DiCamillo), I asked, "So how is your classroom library going?"

"Good," she responded, without hesitation. "We have some new books to include which will force me to weed out some titles that weren't being read by the kids." I continued with a few more follow-up questions, beating around the bush until I finally asked what I really wanted to know.

"I noticed that you organized the classroom library prior to the students' first day. What are your thoughts on that?" The teacher paused, likely thinking about the best way to respond.

I did not need to bring up that the entire faculty had previously learned about how to co-organize a classroom library with students. We had a lot of success with this schoolwide activity two years ago. So much so that I assumed co-organizing classroom libraries with students had become a part of our culture. It was apparent that was not the case.

"Well," the teacher finally responded, "to be honest, I've been reluctant to reorganize the classroom library, at least with the students."

"Why?" I asked, genuinely curious.

"For one thing, it's a lot of work. It also takes up a ton of time." I nodded. "And the kids we had last year . . . I don't think they could have handled it." I continued to listen and remained silent. "And if I am being *really* honest, a lot of this has to do with control. It's hard to give that up!" After sharing, I paused while noticing her shoulders visibly relaxed, as if a weight had been on them until now.

"I really appreciate your openness," I finally responded. "I would not have asked the questions I did if I didn't value your perspective. If you have moved back toward more teacher-directed classroom libraries, my guess is other teachers have too."

I left the classroom, mentally preparing for our next leadership team meeting.

Getting Specific With Collective Commitments

We might falsely assume as leaders that only the least effective faculty are the ones who resist change the most. Yet what I have learned is even the best teachers can get stuck in their previous ruts without enough time, resources, and support to make change long term.

If the improvement we seek is truly a priority, we will do whatever it takes to see it become embedded and sustainable in our school. When professional learning and subsequent follow-up via instructional walks are not enough, our next step is to develop collective commitments around the change we want to see. This language, discussed in the previous chapter, reduces ambiguity around the practices we believe will help every student learn successfully.

We started as we have before: revisiting our beliefs as well as the current literature on the topic. This process begins at the instructional leadership team level. In the case of classroom libraries, we presented a slide show of our past success along with teacher anecdotes. Those artifacts serve as evidence of our past successes.

We read additional articles and literature on the benefits of involving students in the development of classroom libraries. Beliefs and research that point in the logical direction are difficult to argue with once examined, yet we still spelled out what this can look like in the classroom. Through dialogue and discussion, teacher-leaders and I crafted the following five statements:

1. Classroom libraries should contain a large quantity of books from all genres; texts above, at, and below readability for students in that classroom.

2. Classroom libraries are accessible to all students and organized in such a way that all students are able to "shop" for books that are good-fit books—that is, in terms of readability and interest.

3. Classroom libraries are diverse. See NCTE's position statement for a definition of diverse (ncte.org/statement/classroom-libraries).

4. Portions of the library are investigated by students *and* teacher(s) to learn about the books. This may be done at the beginning of the year, throughout the year, and/or when it fits into the natural curriculum.

5. Students participate in display and/or organization, such as changing book displays, including students' choice of books, and weeding or analyzing the condition of the books and collections.

These commitments were presented in draft form to the faculty. We sought consensus on each statement. Time was provided to ask questions and clarify the meaning of the language. Then, using a Google Form, teachers selected on a scale of 1 to 5, with 5 being full commitment and 1 being no commitment, to each statement. See our results in Table 4.1.

Table 4.1 Teachers' level of commitment to classroom libraries

Statement	Average rating
Classroom libraries should contain a large quantity of books from all genres: texts above, at, and below readability for students in that classroom.	4.71
Classroom libraries are accessible to all students and organized in such a way that all students are able to "shop" for books that are good-fit books—that is, in terms of readability and interest.	4.76
Classroom libraries are diverse. (See NCTE's position statement for a definition of diverse.)	4.65
Portions of the library are investigated by students *and* teacher(s) to learn about the books. This may be done at the beginning of the year, throughout the year, and/or when it fits into the natural curriculum.	4.47
Students participate in display and/or organization, such as changing book displays, including students' choice of books, and weeding or analyzing the condition of the books and collections.	3.53

When I present these results to other school leaders during a conference session or workshop, I ask them what they notice and what their theory is. The lower score on the last statement calls their attention. Theories they have shared include the following:

▶ Teachers do not want to give up control of their classroom.

▶ Teachers are worried about the kids making a mess.

▶ They are giving up a lot of time by doing this, especially if they have a lot of books.

I have also added that, in our culture of judgment, faculty feel an overwhelming sense of urgency to get results in reading and other areas. It is easier to set up the classroom library and get engaged with instruction right away when our system values test scores more than teaching students lifelong skills such as how to find a good book, manage a community, or connect with others over a love for literature.

We can combat this culture by continuing to recognize and reinforce our long-term goals: that of student and teacher independence and interdependence, most readily supported when we approach our educational experiences with a coaching and supportive stance.

WISDOM FROM THE FIELD: HOW TO TIE YOUR SHOES

UCLA (University of California-Los Angeles) men's basketball coach Jon Wooden would teach his players the proper way to tie their shoes before playing. Pull up your socks and leave no loose flaps inside your sneakers. This was his first lesson of the year. "He didn't want blisters," former player Rich Levin recalled. "I mean, that's not a serious illness, but you could miss a game or two" (Vecsey, 2010).

What small skill or strategy could you commit to learning as a faculty that would make a big difference for your student learning priority? Who might teach it? Jot down some ideas and thoughts in your journal.

BACK IN THE CLASSROOM

After the collective commitment process, I checked in with the teacher, with whom I realized that classroom libraries were not fully implemented as originally planned.

Our conversation felt more relaxed, like a brainstorming session. I chalked it up to the clarity we had created around the expectations. "Should I start over?" she asked, gesturing toward the nicely organized classroom library.

I paused to think before responding, noting she had asked me for my opinion so I had an invitation to communicate feedback. "That seems like a lot of work. What if you were simply honest with your students about your concerns? Maybe frame it as an inquiry project and ask them for their input for improving what you already have developed."

She liked that idea. From there we co-developed two big questions to share with the class:

➤ "Do you like how the classroom library is currently organized?"

➤ "What would you change to improve it?"

No promises were made by the teacher. "We'll see how I feel about this tomorrow," the teacher commented, with a slight smile as I left the classroom.

CONCLUSION: YOU HAVE TO FOCUS ON SOMETHING

In my previous building, we became a "lab school," in which our classrooms would open for colleagues from other districts to observe and learn.

During our first visit, one consultant from our state's Department of Public Instruction was in attendance. As we walked the halls with the visiting school, noticing all the writing hanging up, I asked the consultant if she had noticed any patterns or trends among other lab schools.

"You don't all focus on the same thing. Some schools prioritize student intervention services, others on mathematics. But you all focus on one thing."

Organizing around a priority is not as easy as it might seem. You devote less attention to some aspects of your school and trust that they will still be managed. Focusing on one initiative can start to become boring over time without clear stepping stones—for example, classroom libraries—toward an anticipated goal. Yet the power of situating your collective attention toward a task cannot be understated. By selecting the right focus, supported long term with instructional walks and a coaching stance, many other areas of schools start to feel the positive effect. We will see that in the next chapter, when we begin to affirm all the promising practices that present themselves in the classroom.

SUCCESS INDICATORS FOR ORGANIZING AROUND A PRIORITY

- You can ask almost any faculty member in your school what your focus is at that current time, and they can articulate the priority. This includes describing what it is and why it is the focus.

- Other subject areas and general school conditions begin to benefit from a singular focus. With the example of classroom libraries, in addition to reading achievement and engagement improved, teachers noticed students were more apt to write, especially about their reading.

- Purchasing requests and classroom budgets will more likely align with what your school deems as a priority. Because you started by examining your beliefs, teachers have hopefully considered new possibilities for the focus.

- There likely is resistance from a few faculty members to the new initiative. That is not necessarily a bad thing. It surfaces a few issues. First, that the priority is clear (a teacher cannot adequately explain why they disagree with a commitment if they do not understand it). Second, this can be an opportunity for collaborative inquiry, in which we can resist getting into a battle of wills and instead ask clarifying questions—for instance, "What specifically about co-organizing classroom libraries do you take issue with?" By approaching these challenges with curiosity instead of concern, we can find opportunities for success on each teacher's terms.

Reflective Questions

Consider the following questions to promote reflection. You can respond to them in writing and/or in conversation with colleagues.

1. What are three key takeaways for you after reading this chapter?

2. If you had to select two faculty members to be on your instructional leadership team, who would they be? What makes these teachers promising candidates?

3. Consider the data you currently have for your school or district. What one focus do you believe could be the priority for your improvement work? How does the data support it?

5

AFFIRM PROMISING PRACTICES

> *What teachers want more than feedback is for leaders to notice them. They want their instructional leaders to acknowledge their goals, their decisions, and their successes.*
>
> —Baeder (2018, p. 102)

After multiple years of success at my previous school, some staff expressed interest in studying a different approach to literacy instruction. One teacher in our instructional leadership team suggested a structured writing program. We agreed. Classrooms were provided with graphic organizers and routines, part of a program aligned with the Common Core State Standards. Many of the teachers appreciated the structuredness of the tools. And when we implemented the strategies, students' writing volume increased.

However, the preferred results we wanted—engaged, effective writers—did not come about. There was less joy and voice in what the students were saying. They were writing to a standard, but not necessarily with purpose or for an authentic audience. We discovered this the next year during a midyear writing assessment. "Technically, the students can produce great paragraphs," noted one teacher. Another chimed in, "Yeah, but would anyone want to read them?" A few faculty members laughed in acknowledgment.

Speaking with other school leaders, this switching of school initiatives after a year or two is not uncommon. We try one approach out, the initial results may be promising, and yet we go on a hunt for the next best thing. Pretty soon, we forget the shared beliefs we found agreement on in the first place.

A focus on process and investing in teachers' capacity for self-directedness is where our attention is better positioned. After studying two decades of research regarding a school leader's influence on teaching and learning, Grissom et al. (2021) found the following practices to be attributed to a positive impact on students and schools. I have positioned the tenets of this book to show alignment with this study's findings in Table 5.1.

Table 5.1 Research-to-resource comparison

"How Principals Affect Students and Schools" (Grissom et al., 2021)	Leading Like a C.O.A.C.H.
Establish a productive school climate	Create confidence through trust
Manage personnel and resources strategically	Organize around a priority
Focus on high-leverage engagement in instruction, such as through teacher evaluations and coaching	Affirm promising practices; communicate feedback
Facilitate collaboration and professional learning communities	Help teachers become leaders and learners

These practices help teachers become building leaders and lifelong learners, with the ultimate goal of a sustainable, self-determining school. Our most important role as leaders is to develop the leadership capacity of others. Adopting a coaching stance, when appropriate, supports teachers both as leaders and as learners.

WHAT DO YOU MEAN BY BEST PRACTICE?

During a conversation I once had with a district administrator about adopting a scripted curriculum program, their argument was that the resource was based on "best practice." This stance invites resistance. Educational researcher Viviane Robinson (2018) notes that "appeals to adopt 'best practice' imply that current practice is less than best, and such implicit evaluations are more likely to generate mistrust and suspicion than enthusiasm for change" (p. 39).

Related, who gets to determine what a "best practice" is in education? This is a valid question. Education is evolving, considering new research and changing environments, especially with technology. As a colleague noted, "If someone has figured out the best way to teach, everyone would be doing it and education would be fixed." This leads to a raft of problems, not limited to the retroactive guilt teachers might feel from previous teaching decisions and the difficult argument one tries to make in defending their practice.

Both issues surface the reality that teaching is dynamic and holds too many variables to ever deem one teaching practice, resource, or strategy as the epitome of our profession. There will be scenarios in which almost any teaching practice situated in a specific classroom fails to help students learn. For example, feedback may have less of an impact if a relationship has not first been established between a teacher and a student, or the goal for a lesson has not been clearly articulated.

This example confirms the theory of practice described in this very book: that every school already has the professional capacity to address its unique challenges. Yet the last thing I would proclaim is to follow this theory to a "T." No one can possibly know with certainty how teachers will respond to these strategies in your school. While there is "nothing more practical than a good theory," it is only as effective as its flexibility and adaptability to unique situations. Yes, trust is a foundation for this work. Yes, it is hard to move forward together without some type of priority. Yet trust can be fostered in myriad ways. Every school has its own specific needs to prioritize around.

> While there is "nothing more practical than a good theory," it is only as effective as its flexibility and adaptability to unique situations.

So instead of asking you to develop the typical plan, break it down into objectives, and then follow a linear process to success, we are going to remain somewhere between curiosity and certainty by focusing on promising practices in the classroom and how we as leaders can affirm them when we see them during instructional walks.

THREE TENETS OF PROMISING PRACTICES

The construct of "promising practices" strikes me as the right balance between having confidence in our current classroom practice and remaining open to new ways of instruction. It is the paradox of belief: that we have both trust in ourselves and curiosity toward other possibilities.

With that, what makes a practice promising? I see three criteria:

1. *The practice is aligned with the district's vision and a school's shared beliefs:* It is important that whatever teaching strategy, method, or approach is employed schoolwide, that it is coherent with what the faculty believe to be true. For example, in our school we believe that phonemic awareness can be taught with students' own writing. That does not preclude a teacher from using direct instruction of phonics. But if isolated skill development is the only way in which phonemic awareness is developed with students, then that is not a promising practice. Word study removed from an authentic context is not aligned with our beliefs.

2. *The practice has evidence to support its effectiveness:* As a professional, we must look to current research to make an informed decision about what practices enter our curriculum and classrooms. John Hattie (2021) offers a list of the most effective practices (visiblelearning.com) based on a summary of many studies on each approach (a meta-analysis) at his Visible Learning website.

3. *There are situations in which the practice may be ineffective:* This rule would seem to apply to almost any practice in education. For example, summarization has a high impact on student learning. But what text or content are the students being asked to summarize? Is it relevant to their lives, or simply a generic passage assigned by the teacher to address a standard? Furthermore, were students able to select the information that they are to summarize (motivation also has an impact)? In addition, did the teacher engage in some type of shared demonstration of summarization prior to releasing the responsibility?

    Facilitating instruction is not like taking a pill prescribed to you by your doctor; the nuances and variables of teaching and learning are too great to accept any practice as infallible.

So how can we find agreement on anything? By leading like a coach and affirming the process of teaching and learning: noticing and naming what is going well and getting curious about what might need improvement.

AFFIRMATION: NOT JUST A PAT ON THE BACK

One of my favorite Saturday Night Live characters is Stuart Smalley. Played by Al Franken, Smalley hosted a mock talk show even though he was "not a licensed therapist." His daily affirmation was "I am good enough, I am smart enough, and—doggone it—people like me."

While the "Daily Affirmation" show provided many laughs, the actual affirmations were more pats on the back. True affirmations are valid. They are positive-oriented feedback you can substantiate with evidence. They are not a simple "good job." The recipient of an affirmation understands what they did and how it had an impact on student learning.

Merriam-Webster (n.d.) defines the verb "affirm" as the following:

- To validate
- To confirm
- To state positively
- To express a strong *belief* in an idea

All these descriptors point toward an affirmation being dependent on facts. In the context of the classroom, this means evidence documented objectively through an instructional walk.

During my visits, I will typically frame an affirmation at the end of my notes. For example, I observed a reading intervention session for one first-grade student. As the teacher presented her prepared slide with a sentence to dissect, the student brought up an associated idea that surfaced: "Like ants on a log!"

The teacher, not wanting to dismiss his contribution, wrote out his sentence on the board. "Let's study this one together." They took the time to identify the sounds within those words that the student had offered; it became the new content for the skill lesson.

In my notes, I framed my affirmation as follows: "Creating a space for your students to call up and work with their own sources of knowledge makes instruction more meaningful and, ultimately, more effective."

After I gave her my notes and commended Rachael Schroeder (personal communication, April 14, 2021) on the flexibility she displayed, she responded, "That's responsive teaching!"

In a culture that prizes fidelity to a program over responsiveness to the student, this event might have been viewed negatively. There are schools where teachers are reprimanded for deviating from the prescribed curriculum program. Yet if you were to ask the leaders in these organizations what they value, they likely could call up their mission of ensuring every student is successful and cared for.

The lack of coherence between a school's vision and the implementation of their ideals is what occurs when we fail to build trust or focus on a priority. Our actions are driven by external factors instead of what we know to be true for our school. To engage in sustainable change over time, affirming the practices that will likely lead us to improvement is that next step in our professional learning journey.

SPECIAL NOTE: WHEN INSTRUCTION SEEMS TO BE INEFFECTIVE

Even with the most positive of lenses, leaders will walk into classrooms in which the teaching and learning appears less than effective. In these situations, we can take one of two stances during an instructional walk:

- Stick around longer than the normal amount of time of 10-15 minutes. Sometimes it is simply a matter of allowing a lesson to unfold, which can start to reveal positive aspects to notice, name, and reinforce through affirmation.

- Leave the classroom and chalk it up to a lesson that did not go as planned. Every teacher has their off day. That's the beauty of instructional walks: we are in classrooms so frequently that a less than effective lesson is likely an outlier.

Of course, if you start to see a pattern of ineffective instruction in one classroom during instructional walks, this is a cue to engage in your district's teacher evaluation process. (See "Special Note" in Chapter 6.)

FOUR PRINCIPLES FOR INITIATING POSITIVE CHANGE

All living things tend to thrive in positive environments. A plant bends toward the sun and spreads its roots toward sources of water. This concept also applies to people. Costa et al. (2016) found that "ratios of nearly 6 to 1 positive to negative interactions within teams distinguish high-performing groups from mid- to low-performing groups"

(p. 308). As leaders, we can both create the immediate environment for growth via instructional walks and guide a process that creates more positive conditions.

Perkins and Reese (2014) identified four principles for schoolwide change that first builds on educators' strengths and then leverages those points for future growth.

1. Adopt an Instructional Framework

2. Learn With Your Teachers

3. Develop Collaborative Learning Communities

4. Institutionalize Promising Practices

These principles begin a transition in this process, from focusing on the individual teacher to building the capacity of teams and the broader school community to sustain a journey toward excellence for the long term.

PRINCIPLE 1: ADOPT AN INSTRUCTIONAL FRAMEWORK

A framework "offers a vision for more effectively teaching and learning" (Perkins & Reese, 2014). A common trait of instructional frameworks is it "provides teachers with a common perspective and language while allowing adaptation to different subjects, levels, and students" (Perkins & Reese, 2014).

An instructional framework also defines core elements of the approach. The definition need not be too specific; all teachers can see their current practices approximating toward more effective approaches. As Perkins and Reese (2014) ask, "Does the framework make room for individual teacher styles and commitments, so that most teachers can come to 'own' it over time?"

An instructional framework does not necessarily have to come from outside the school culture, although that can be helpful when getting started. If a school is confident in the priority and has established trust building-wide, developing a framework internally can bring about more ownership.

For example, during the 2020-2021 school year when we were managing instruction during the pandemic, we used feedback from our families to develop an instructional framework. We analyzed comments from a survey about the previous spring's remote learning experience:

what worked and what needed improvement. From that information, we were able to develop a framework consisting of five different areas:

1. *Authenticity:* Real-world tasks and mistakes encouraged as part of learning

2. *Being Clear:* Multiple ways of explaining concepts, often through shared experiences

3. *Communication:* Proactive, using multiple modes and entry points

4. *Discussion:* Student-centered, around important texts and topics

5. *Empowerment:* Voice and choice in what students would learn, and trying to build on their interests

Our previous framework had 10 different elements. We reduced it to five to keep our work simple in those complex times. Like the previous framework, these elements were aligned with our shared beliefs and our priority. The descriptions were specific enough that we could achieve some level of coherence across classrooms, yet flexible so every teacher could align their own practice with it.

ACTIVITY 5.1 — ADOPT OR DEVELOP AN INSTRUCTIONAL FRAMEWORK

To further clarify promising practices beyond collective commitments, have your instructional leadership team explore and eventually agree on an instructional framework. Align the language with the current needs of your school.

A question comes up at this point: Should we create our own or adopt an instructional framework developed by an outside party? My suggestion is as follows:

- If you are just beginning with a schoolwide initiative, *adopt an instructional framework*. Learn the language that others have developed, educators who have traveled down a similar road to your journey.

- If you have a history of clear successes as a school, consider *adapting or developing your own instructional framework*. Your culture likely has more confidence in what you are already doing, so keep that momentum going forward. Delve into the current research on the initiative you want to explore and summarize what's promising for that area of instruction.

In either situation, we have now shifted the onus of expertise from you as a leader with a limited perspective to a more objective description of what your culture believes will lead to schoolwide excellence. (*Suggestion:* Analyze the alignment between the framework and your teacher's evaluation rubric. Faculty will sometimes use instructional walks as artifacts for their professional portfolios.)

EXAMPLE 5.1: AUTHENTICITY IN WRITERS WORKSHOP

In my previous school during an instructional walk, I caught myself making assumptions within moments of entering the classroom. A letter writing template was posted on the board. Much of the text was provided; students needed to fill in only a few words.

Two of my assumptions were the following:

- It is January; students should be more independent by this time.
- Related, the teacher's expectations may not be high enough.

These are judgments and are grounded in my limited beliefs and lack of context. So I withheld in making any inferences and, again, looked for what was going well. There was much to appreciate:

- Students who were finished with their writing were reading independently.
- Many of the books the students were reading came from the classroom library.
- They had self-selected their own titles to read on their own.
- There was an authentic audience for their letter writing (thank you note for the classroom gifts they received as part of a collaborative digital project).
- The teacher had previously partnered with the library media specialist on the collaborative digital project, which led to the letter writing.
- Shared writing was utilized by the teacher to demonstrate the process.

Some of these observations echoed previous classroom visits and the subsequent conversations with the teacher. Knowing all of the positives that had led up to today, I asked the following question to learn more about the lesson: "I noticed that much of the letter content was provided. How did you determine how much scaffolding the students needed for writing the letter?"

She responded, "We have not spent enough time on writing letters, so I thought it would be better if we did this one with a lot of support. We really wanted our letters to look sharp for our community members who donated to our project."

(Continued)

(Continued)

After more discussion about this activity. I thanked her for sharing this background with me. As well, I acknowledged her desire for working toward craftsmanship and instilling this trait with her kids. What I did not do at that time was to ask when the kids would be ready to write letters independently. That would come next time, during future visits. Instead, in my instructional walk notes that I handed to her, I circled "authenticity" within the affixed framework we had adopted for the year. "Thank you for giving kids an audience and a real-world task," I shared as I left the classroom.

ACTIVITY 5.2 — ASK QUESTIONS USING LANGUAGE FROM YOUR INSTRUCTIONAL FRAMEWORK

My goal in inquiring with teachers about their practice is not to interrogate their work. What I want is to first understand their thinking and the choices that went into the lesson.

Positioning these questions within the context of our framework language during instructional walks helps draw teachers' attention to our focus. The questions posed use evidence from what was observed and aligned with promising practices.

Baeder (2018) offers a list of questions to ask during classroom visits that can help teachers reflect on what they are doing and why they are doing it. Here is a sample (pp. 105-106):

- "I noticed that you _____. Could you talk to me about how that fits within this lesson or unit?"
- "Here's what I saw: _____. How does that compare with what you thought was happening at the time?"
- "I noticed that _____. How did you feel about how that went?"
- "Tell me about when you _____. What made you choose that response?"

Next is the question from the previous example. Notice the inclusion of "scaffolding" and the focus on writing.

"I noticed that much of the letter content was provided. How did you determine how much scaffolding the students needed for writing the letter?"

The teacher and I had clarity around the terms and built trust through prior positive interactions. Now we could engage in a coaching conversation, including the follow-up affirmation of her decision making. This work is centered on the process of improving.

During your classroom visits, ask questions of teachers based on their own goals and the instructional framework.

PRINCIPLE 2: LEARN WITH YOUR TEACHERS

Some debate still surrounds the best approach to leadership. What we know right now to be a promising practice is for school leaders to engage in professional learning with teachers. To engage, in this context means both to lead and to participate in professional development.

Robinson (2018), citing a previous study she had been involved in, compared different styles of school leadership using previous studies to create a meta-analysis. She found that, of the five most effective actions an instructional leader can display, "promoting and participating in teacher learning and development" (p. 10) had the largest effect size (0.84). It means that leaders who are "actively involved with their teachers as the 'leading learners' of their school" (Robinson et al., 2008, p. 663) can double their impact on student learning in comparison to other practices deemed effective or having at least one year's worth of growth in one year.

What does "actively involved" mean? The researchers highlight that leaders who make an impact will engage in "informal staff discussions of teaching and teaching problems" (Robinson et al., 2008, p. 663). This participation in dialogue about practice leads teachers to view their leaders as "both more accessible and more knowledgeable about instructional matters than their counterparts in otherwise similar lower achieving schools" (Robinson et al., 2008, p. 663).

How this learning process rolls out in a school varies. The principal can be heavily involved in leading formal professional learning, or they can be primarily a participant while designated faculty facilitates the professional development sessions. Perkins and Reese (2014) advocate for the latter. They differentiate between *political* and *practical visionaries.*

- School leaders serve as political visionaries, showing "conspicuous commitment to the innovation, advocating it, making it a priority, defending it against critics, explaining it to parents, appearing for key events, and allocating resources."

- Practical visionaries are "sometimes a team of two or three teachers" who "manages the program on the ground, organizing faculty groups and events and conducting some training and coaching." If this is the approach taken, it is important that teacher-leaders "have significant time formally allocated" to prepare and guide this professional learning.

For example, when I first began as principal at my previous school, the lead interventionist oversaw the monthly learning sessions on the reading-writing connection. It was a helpful experience for me, as I could build trust and clarify the priority by engaging in professional dialogue with faculty. Then when I was in the classrooms, there was a natural transition, from learning together something new to discussing the implementation of these strategies in real time during an instructional walk.

EXAMPLE 5.2: ACTION RESEARCH IN A SECONDARY LITERACY INTERVENTION

In my previous district, we partnered with a state university to offer teachers action research as a professional learning opportunity. Faculty members from several schools elected to develop a driving question around their instruction, implement a plan for trying a new practice, collect and analyze data, and hopefully improve in their work.

I served as a political visionary, such as by communicating the importance of this work to district staff and families. The two university professors who facilitated the action research were the practical visionaries—for example, leading the study sessions.

Yet even in this situation I was able to find opportunities to take a coaching stance with staff. For example, secondary literacy interventionist Mary Beth Nicklaus (personal communication, May 31, 2016) wanted to know how to help her students see reading as something you do outside of school. "One of my students is more interested in hunting." She brought in literature involving the outdoors, but no luck. Many of her students lacked the necessary series of past successes to be confident readers.

Mary Beth hypothesized that if she wrote about her own life in front of her students, especially about her own struggles, that they might see literacy as a lifelong activity, something they could engage in beyond the school walls. So she began journaling and projecting her writing onto the whiteboard while the students watched. For example, Mary Beth wrote about the time she bought four Pop-Tarts at the snack station after a bad day. "I saw you buy those Pop-Tarts," one girl shared.

The vulnerability Mary Beth displayed gave students permission to also be open about their own struggles. Pretty soon students were engaging in independent reading, with Mary Beth's careful modeling of her own reading life plus her guidance and support. Over the course of the year, students were starting to exit out of her intervention due to excellent reading progress, but they did not want to leave. She had created a safe learning space, and it started with her. "I had to change my own mindset to change theirs."

After I learned about her experience, I commented that the professional learning we had engaged in in my own school used shared reading and shared writing. "We see similar enthusiasm for literacy," I added. Mary Beth was excited to know that other teachers were using authentic approaches to their instruction. I shared some of our resources with her.

ACTIVITY 5.3 COMMIT TO PROFESSIONAL READING AND LEARNING

Beyond speaking directly with experts in the field, there is no more effective or efficient way to stay current than professional reading. Books, journals, and reliable digital content immerse us in the specific terminology of our complex profession. Next is a suggested list of professional learning opportunities that you can begin tomorrow.

- *Leadership and Discipline-Specific Literature:* This can happen independently or with a book club. When reading, consider writing brief responses to the information in the margins, almost as if you are having a conversation with the author. Dog-ear pages that you want to come back to in the future, such as when preparing professional development. Share favorite quotes and passages with colleagues to sustain a culture of learning, such as in your newsletter.

- *Journals, Research Summaries:* Favorite leadership journals include *Phi Delta Kappan* and *Educational Leadership*. Because of my school's commitment to literacy instruction, I currently subscribe to International Literacy Association's *Reading Research Quarterly* and *The Reading Teacher*, National Council of Teachers of English's *Language Arts* and *Voices From the Middle*, and my state's reading association's quarterly journal (Wisconsin State Reading Association). I do not read every article; I will preview the table of contents and select one or two pieces. These journals fit nicely in my padfolio. If I encounter a pause during my classroom visits or between instructional walks, I can pull out a journal and read during this time.

- *Blogs, Newsletters, and Social Media:* I recommend this source of information while acknowledging there is no one editing the content for validity or bias. That said, many ideas shared in these online spaces are worth your attention. For myself, I read what colleagues share on Twitter. As well, I subscribe to several leadership or literacy blogs and newsletters—for example, Choice Literacy (Full disclosure: I am currently a contributor). Relevant content is delivered right to my inbox.

You might ask, *when do I have time to read during the school day?* Like anything that is a priority: schedule it. I put time for professional reading in my calendar under "IL Review" (IL stands for instructional leadership). Close the door and devote some time to self-study. Although I advocate for more time, engaging in professional reading for even one hour a week will make a difference in your knowledge base.

PRINCIPLE 3: DEVELOP COLLABORATIVE LEARNING COMMUNITIES

The advantages of professional learning communities do not end with teachers working together on problems of practice. This setup also gives leaders the opportunity to apply coaching skills by leveraging the power of the group.

Kim and Gonzales-Black (2018) recognize that professional growth within schools occurs most readily with teams: "As organizations implement practices that require more responsiveness, quicker alignment, and faster decision making, teams—not autocratic bosses—are becoming the units of change in organizations" (p. 35). A key to developing productive teams is giving them tools to become collaborative and focused on learning from each other.

The skills involved in leading like a coach are just as applicable to teachers with colleagues. These "collaborative norms" (Costa et al., 2016) support dialogue that helps teachers talk about their challenges and be more receptive to new ideas, especially described via the promising practices defined within an instructional framework.

Implementing these "rules for engagement" serves as a professional scaffold for the collaborative conversations. Teachers within any building are at different levels of capacity; even when trust is high and the priority is clear, conflict is still common. As Perkins and Reese (2014) note, "any widespread innovation in a school involves a tapestry of interactions within the community of teachers, school leaders, and beyond. We have never seen all members of such a community energetically and uniformly invest themselves in a new change initiative." Once we recognize the complexities of instructional improvement, we can better plan for this process.

O.W.N.: A Protocol for Collaboration

I have developed the process "O.W.N." after years of observing and working with teachers and teams. It stands for the following:

▶ Observations

▶ Wonderings

▶ Next Step

It is a routine initially designed based on instructional walks. (In fact, you can utilize this routine for classroom visits if you feel you need more of a scaffold.) This process is used as a way of documenting teaching and learning and then analyzing trends and patterns about instruction over time. It takes the form of an "instructional letter" (Baeder, 2018).

To start, I will reread my scanned-in notes from classroom visits for a certain team, say over the past two months. Then I will list on the top of my letter what *observations* were made that are aligned with the promising practices we have been learning about as a school.

For example, I visited all three of our four-year-old kindergarten classrooms. The teachers have been embedding language instruction within the concept of play. In one classroom, they created a pretend ice rink. Prior to participating in this center, the class engaged in a whole-group discussion about the items and actions that will be a part of the experience. One observation I noted was the authenticity of the activity that incorporated the vocabulary for the point of interest.

After several strengths-focused observations, I posed a *wondering*. It delves deeper into the observations. These questions are genuine inquiries. I try to avoid leading questions that would guide teachers toward any preferred destination. (The acronym "O.W.N." is also a reminder to me to ensure that teachers are ultimately the point of authority in this collaborative process.)

With the four-year-old kindergarten example, I offered the following question: "The language skills are embedded in play. How much or how little do you name these skills during instruction?"

One teacher responded by acknowledging that she will sometimes make a point to name these teaching points, "but at this age, much of it would be above them, and I also do not want to distract them from the enjoyment of the experience." I nodded, affirming her rationale, which was now available for both of us to understand.

Finally, there is a space for a possible *next step*. These possibilities are generated by the teams themselves. Using the O.W.N. protocol, my intention is to gradually release the thinking process to the faculty. My role is to hand the proverbial pen over to them so they can reach conclusions about future actions to take in their professional learning.

To continue the present example, the four-year-old kindergarten teachers brought up their interest in play planning. "Should we start having our kids draw out or even write out their goal for their time in the center?" Discussion followed, with some concerns around whether play planning might reduce the creativity in their learning. "This is an interesting question," I affirmed. After a pause without a response, I posed the following question: "We want to know if too much structure might reduce students' sense of play. Any thoughts on how we could assess this during play planning?"

This was a more guided question, but I felt it was appropriate as I sensed some uncertainty in direction. They agreed. One suggestion was to capture images and videos as a way to assess students' progress for learning over time in these areas. "We can post them on Seesaw (a digital family communications platform) so parents can also see their kids improve during the school year." Now my role during future classroom visits became more focused: I could attend to this new approach of assessing play planning during centers.

EXAMPLE 5.3: FOURTH GRADE FACILITATING STUDENT DISCUSSION

I emailed the fourth-grade team: "Would you have a chance for me during professional learning community time to share a few things I have noticed during instructional walks?" I had recently completed two rounds of classroom visits and read my notes. "Stop by tomorrow," they responded.

I first started with my observations, again: strengths-oriented and aligned with our instructional framework (in bold).

- Expectations for student **independence**
- Inclusion of students' interests/suggestions for classroom library
- Clear **demonstrations** of skills and strategies
- Responding to students' needs in the moment
- Diverse literature and integration with content areas
- Celebrating student accomplishments and milestones

Thinking about one element of our instructional framework for promoting equity—student discussion—I posed the following wondering: "I noticed students are primarily located at desks. Given this arrangement, how do you manage and facilitate student discussion?"

I paused. The team was silent for a few moments. Then a teacher responded, "One thing I have found effective is 'neighborhood sharing' to support student discussion." The teacher went on to explain how this structure for discussion asked that students quickly position their desks to face each other. Then they each take a turn sharing their thinking, with everyone getting a chance to offer their ideas before transitioning to a more natural conversation. "That way, each student's voice is heard."

The rest of the team responded positively. ("Oh, I like that term, 'neighborhood sharing'. It seems very inclusive.") The rest of our discussion led to possible next steps, written down for future application.

WISDOM FROM THE FIELD: HOW GOOGLE BUILT A BETTER TEAM

Google wanted to learn more about teamwork for better collaboration. The technology company studied what the best groups in their organization did to be successful. They found that "understanding and influencing group norms were the keys to improving Google's teams." More specifically, teams that supported equity in voices heard (i.e., taking turns) and were skilled at perceiving how others felt were most effective (Duhigg, 2016).

How might O.W.N. and other protocols help develop positive group norms and practices? What is your role as a leader in modeling and monitoring effective collaboration? Jot down some ideas and thoughts in your journal.

PRINCIPLE 4: INSTITUTIONALIZE PROMISING PRACTICES

The goal of leading like a coach is nurturing self-directed leaders and learners among your staff: developing a school culture that can sustain itself beyond one's tenure. Your organization is a system and a community, with each person and their actions influencing one another. This awareness along with more intention can be achieved by institutionalizing practices found to be most promising for our students, while developing teachers' capacity for collaboration and continuous improvement.

> *Institutionalization as a term might have negative connotations in other contexts, but for getting a school to agree on what works for our kids, it is a critical step for achieving equity.*

To institutionalize means to "stabilize a successful innovation for the long term" (Perkins & Reese, 2014). The beliefs and practices become a part of a culture. They are "the way we do things around here." Everyone owns them.

Teachers and I arrived at our beliefs and practices collaboratively. They were not imposed on us from a district or state mandate. We moved toward our approach together. *Institutionalization* as a term might have negative connotations in other contexts, but for getting a school to agree on what works for our kids, it is a critical step for achieving equity.

EXAMPLE 5.4: ANALYZING SCHOOLWIDE ENGAGEMENT

How do we find agreement? It first begins with awareness. Think back to some of the instructional walk examples shared in this chapter:

- A writing session with scaffolding
- A responsive reading intervention lesson
- An intermediate team's efforts in promoting student discussion

These experiences initially appear disparate and without connection. What they have in common is they were all aligned with our instructional framework. We can use frameworks to identify trends and patterns in schoolwide instruction. This information can be presented visually to an instructional leadership team to inform decision making about professional development and building goals.

For example, one year at my previous school we agreed to focus on student engagement. After reading several articles on the topic, we came up with the following attributes:

- Student Choice
- Relevance

- Scaffolding
- Group Discussion
- Questioning
- Motivation
- Authenticity
- Integration
- Clarity
- Feedback

In my subsequent instructional walks, I noted what tenet of our framework was most evident in each classroom after a visit. After about 100 walks, I compiled the results to analyze trends and patterns in what I was observing. These results would eventually be shared with the faculty in a visual format (Figure 5.1).

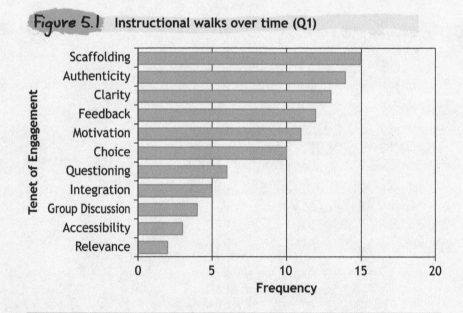

Figure 5.1   Instructional walks over time (Q1)

In this example, I noticed after the first 100 walks that scaffolding, authenticity, and clarity of instruction were frequently observed. Conversely, higher-order questioning and group discussion were infrequent.

(Continued)

(Continued)

During an instructional leadership team meeting, a few teachers offered reasons why questioning and discussion were low. "We have so much to cover during the school year—we don't have time to stop, ask questions, and discuss!" I listened but would not commit to any statement. Instead, I would pose questions. "Thinking about your upcoming units of study, where might you find opportunities for students to ask questions and to discuss?" This would be followed up with time for teachers to talk about this with colleagues during professional learning sessions.

The next 100 walks revealed changes in teachers' instruction. Group discussion was more frequently observed (Figure 5.2).

We celebrated this accomplishment. It was noted by a teacher that questioning was still not happening with regularity. We agreed that more professional development on how to incorporate higher-order questioning within instruction would be appreciated in the future.

Figure 5.2 Instructional walks over time (Q2)

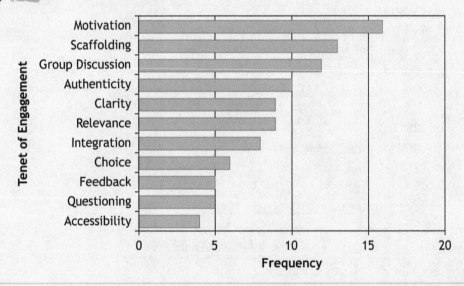

ACTIVITY 5.4 — VISIT CLASSROOMS IN GRADE LEVEL/ DEPARTMENT CLUSTERS

Plan instructional walks so you visit one team or department at roughly the same time. Baeder (2018) notes, "You'll learn much more about the curriculum, shared practices, and assessments that a team or department uses when you visit every member of the group in succession. The more context you can gain by visiting other teachers in the same grade or department, the richer your conversations with teachers can be" (p. 37).

If each instructional walk takes about 15 minutes, you can reasonably visit three classrooms in an hour. It will be a unique experience in each classroom, but you may see some of the same promising practices employed in similar environments. This broader context gives leaders a more complete perspective of instruction for that team. This information can positively influence both individual and team conversations later.

Baeder (2018) also notes that scheduling these visits concurrently within a grade level or department helps ensure better perceptions around equity of professional supervision with instructional walks—any one individual teacher will not feel singled out.

To help ensure you are visiting classrooms in grade level/department clusters, I organize all my teachers on a spreadsheet in their respective teams. This spreadsheet is used to note which tenet of the instructional framework was observed and to quickly see who I need to visit next to achieve a broader understanding.

CONCLUSION: PROFESSIONAL LEARNING THROUGH CONVERSATION

After our midyear writing assessment revealed that our structured writing program may be inhibiting student voice, the leadership team met again to discuss next steps. The conversation was brief. We acknowledged some of the tools that we learned and would like to hold onto. But the consensus was clear: authenticity was necessary, especially when developing a purpose and an audience for writing.

While it was important that we learned what was working and what we needed to change, we also realized we were better able to have a conversation about our practices and the resources we used openly. There was less judgment or blame. Even if we could have made better decisions, we had established trust prior to this open dialogue. Also, having a priority led to the adoption of an instructional framework to ensure alignment between our school district's mission, our beliefs, and what we were attempting to implement.

Yet what if we had known this prior to a schoolwide assessment? Could there have been anything done in the classroom during instructional walks to provide information more quickly about the initiative? Looking back, I think I could have better communicated feedback about the process.

SUCCESS INDICATORS FOR AFFIRMING PROMISING PRACTICES

- Teachers may ask you more often to visit and observe a lesson, or maybe an outcome of their instruction.

- What was once new will become a normal part of the everyday learning experience.

- Teachers will innovate with the promising practices once they become proficient in using them.

- Your better teachers may become complacent with affirmations only and will ask for more critical feedback from you. This is a positive sign and the topic of the next chapter.

Reflective Questions

Consider the following questions to promote reflection. You can respond to them in writing and/or in conversation with colleagues.

1. What are three key takeaways for you after reading this chapter?

2. What two promising instructional practices do you believe could be implemented schoolwide in your building? What evidence supports your belief?

3. If you had to either select a currently available instructional framework or develop one with your teacher-leaders, which option would you choose? Why?

COMMUNICATE FEEDBACK

6

When leaders frame their critical evaluations as definitive and certain, engagement becomes irrelevant because they are convinced they are right. The other person becomes an object for persuasion to one's own point of view, and the dilemma is how to do that without too much upset. Whether the avoidance or judgmental strategy is used, each is disrespectful. Respect requires the elimination of the certainty and judgmental language, together with genuine interest in the other's evaluative stance.

—Robinson (2018, p. 61)

I once administered a survey asking faculty which type of interaction they preferred with me: informal conversations, instructional walks, or formal observations. I was surprised to see this—instructional walks were not their top choice.

As I read the comments, it became clear: some teachers wanted feedback that helped them grow. Not just a description of their practice and how it affected their students but also ideas for improvement.

Why was I not more critical? I wondered. I thought back to a few recent instances in which I had attempted to offer suggestions for improvement. It had not gone well.

How do we communicate feedback in a way that teachers hear it, consider it, and then act on it? Working with other leaders, I believe this is one of the most challenging parts of school leadership. We want change, but we are not sure how to go about it on an individual level, particularly with our more reluctant staff. This chapter offers a pathway toward success in communicating feedback to teachers.

DEFINING FEEDBACK

The most basic understanding of feedback comes from our actions with the world. We receive information all the time. If I am playing a guitar, and I pluck the string, I should hear a sound. It may be off tune, or it may be right on pitch. Either way that sound, a response to my action, is feedback. I can now use that information to make future decisions, such as to keep playing or to tune my guitar.

Feedback between two people or received by one person in an environment (like a classroom) is more difficult to communicate. People are complex. For the recipient of feedback, they have different "lenses" in which they perceive the world. Much of this is based on our beliefs about how things operate and how we exist within an environment.

I now believe that understanding is developed, not delivered. Learning is a collaborative process. And yet this stance can also be problematic as I am now in a position of offering feedback as a leader. Does the potential recipient share a similar view of education? For example, might they take the concept of "teacher" too seriously, in that kids can learn little without their guidance? Feedback can fall on deaf ears if we are not first attuned to both our own and others' belief systems.

So, to communicate feedback, we need to better understand the context in which it is conveyed. For example, if there is any "downside" to developing trust or affirming promising practices, it is that we build positive professional relationships with teachers. So, when we have more critical feedback about their work, we may become concerned about harming that relationship.

Communicating feedback could be compared with tightrope walking: balancing between affirmation and critique of teachers' instruction. We try to maintain balance, not going too far to one side or the other to avoid falling off. Too much affirmation, and teachers start to question your genuineness as a leader. Too much critique, and teachers feel underappreciated.

The bottom line is teachers need information about their practice to grow. If it is unavailable, they may assume everything is working, or they might seek feedback that confirms their biases. As Costa et al. (2016) note, "People need feedback so desperately that, in the absence of actual feedback, they will invent it" (p. 53). It seems to benefit leaders and teachers to at least engage in providing data to support professional improvement, even if we risk getting it wrong.

COMMUNICATING FEEDBACK THROUGH ENGAGEMENT (VS. BYPASS)

We can communicate feedback that can challenge, in a healthy way, teachers' current beliefs and theories, which leads to improvement.

Viviane Robinson, an educational researcher, has found that leaders tend to bypass opportunities for feedback because they do not know how to engage in this process. The solution? Once again, by implementing coaching skills as tools for engagement. These skills, such as paraphrasing and posing questions, have the dual effect of opening our own minds up to possibilities in the classroom while increasing teachers' capacity to view their practice from another perspective.

To facilitate teacher improvement, Robinson (2018) notes that we need to understand classroom actions "from the perspective of the implementing agent" (p. xvi).

Inquiring in the moment is not the only opportunity to understand a teacher's perspective. Through our constant commitment to visiting classrooms and documenting teaching and learning through instruction walks, we end up with many artifacts to help inform us about teachers' theories about their practice. Their decisions and the environment they create are their beliefs-in-action: their values. The leader's role then is not so much about collecting data about teachers' practice but about using that information to communicate feedback in a way that teachers hear it, own it, and use it.

The leader's role is not so much about collecting data about teachers' practice but about using that information to communicate feedback in a way that teachers hear it, own it, and use it.

DIFFERENTIATING FEEDBACK TO MEET TEACHERS' NEEDS

Each educator is unique along their professional learning journey. This includes how they best receive feedback to improve.

For example, Drago-Severson and Blum-DeStefano (2016) found through studies that a developmental approach to feedback increases the likelihood that a teacher will accept information about their practice. They refer to this approach as "feedback for growth" (p. 2). Specifically, they suggest leaders differentiate feedback for four different "ways of knowing" that people tend to fall under (pp. 65-69):

1. *Instrumental:* A need to understand the rules and getting things "right"

2. *Socializing:* Internalizing others' assessments and ensuring others value them

3. *Self-authoring:* Listening to others' beliefs while holding firm to one's own values

4. *Self-transforming:* Seeking growth through reflection and from external feedback

Learning more about each person's ways of knowing, and then accepting where they currently are, is more important than getting our point across, being "right," or exerting control over the situation. Knowledge about teachers' theories is the key to communicating feedback. It helps our faculty hear what we are trying to convey. Drago-Severson and Blum-DeStafano (2016) describe this experience with the metaphor of a radio being "tuned in" (p. 6) to the right station.

It cannot be said enough: this is complex work. To help differentiate and personalize our approach, a "map" is suggested here to communicate feedback more effectively. It can serve as a thinking routine for teachers to include in their own repertoire for self-assessing their own practice. In Chapter 5, I offered this routine for engaging in these types of conversations: O.W.N., or *observations, wonderings,* and *next steps.* It is a process that has surfaced from experience that can help a leader understand a teacher's existing theory of practice. It allows both the leader and the teacher to examine each other's perspectives, a prerequisite for introducing new approaches to existing challenges. See Figure 6.1 for a visual representation of this process.

Three points need to be made here. First, the nonlinear and circuitous nature of the figure represents not only this map but also the nature of feedback. We are in a constant state of dialogue with our teachers. We may start with our observations, such as paraphrasing what we hear teachers say and what we observe, as well as pausing to allow for both parties to process what was currently shared and heard. Yet during the next conversation, a leader and a teacher may begin with the question

Figure 6.1 Engaging in feedback conversations

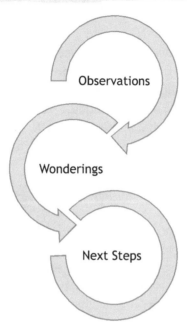

posed during the previous one. This is continuous learning: instead of a beginning or an end, a constant stance toward what beliefs and practices might show promise for increased student learning.

Second, the difference between the wonderings posed in this stage compared with affirming promising practices is whether the questions communicated here seek to create a space between teachers and their current theories. We want to offer a different perspective and, hopefully, create a new theory about how to approach classroom instruction. Previously, we were inquiring into the current thinking behind why teachers are doing what they are doing. Both are important for leading like a coach, yet there is a clear distinction.

➤ Affirming promising practices is focused on strengthening the relationship between teachers' actions and what we believe is most effective for student learning. This originates from the observer/leader.

➤ Communicating feedback is focused on introducing data that may question current theories. This leads to the consideration of new approaches that may not have yet been considered by the teacher but can come from either party.

Finally, the acronym O.W.N. conveys the goal of a leader: to develop the capacity of the teacher to facilitate their own professional learning journey.

The next examples provide three distinct scenarios: a beginning teacher's challenges with classroom management, a more experienced teacher's challenge with innovating within their team, and a veteran teacher's dilemma regarding technology integration. Each coaching conversation is broken down into the O.W.N. map. While names and specific details are changed to respect anonymity, these are real interactions with faculty.

The context for these conversations is as follows:

1. Individual conferences are scheduled with teachers three times a year: fall, winter, and spring. These check-ins take about 20 minutes and give us the space to engage in deeper conversation. In these examples, we are seeing a winter conference, after several walks have been conducted.

2. My written observations from instructional walks are used as evidence to support our conversation, to both affirm what is going well in relation to promising practices and to communicate feedback for growth. Prior to meeting, I reread the scanned copies of my walks along with any additional notes I wrote within their digital folder.

3. The goal is for the teacher to drive the conversation. While leading like a coach, I attempt to guide us toward more effective approaches, but the preferred outcome is typically determined by them.

How do we get there? Again, through using key coaching skills:

▶ Paraphrasing (summarizing in our own words what was heard, clarifying what was shared, organizing a person's thinking for them, or increasing/decreasing the specificity of the conversation)

▶ Pausing (providing time for both parties to process what was said, as well as being aware of our own breathing and body language along with the teacher's)

➤ Posing Questions (seeking to mediate another person's thinking through open-ended and genuinely curious wonderings)

ACTIVITY 6.1 — PREPARE INITIAL COACHING CONVERSATIONS

It takes several opportunities to successfully engage in professional dialogue with the focus on both improving instruction and developing the other person's capacity for self-directedness. Ron Lott, trained in Cognitive Coaching, believes a person needs 20 experiences to become proficient in this process.

One way to scaffold the experience is to prepare a wondering for an upcoming conversation. It can be based on what you previously observed. This is a temporary strategy that can help build initial confidence. Consider initially selecting teachers that you trust to be effective partners in this work.

Preparing a wondering can be based on the data collected in the observations via instructional walks. These wonderings may cause the other person to think about their practice in new ways. Costa et al. (2016) refer to these as "mediative questions" in that they "cause the coachee to supply the data from her own internal and external observations" (p. 53). When leading like a coach in this manner, the goal is not just to improve performance; it is also to build the cognitive capacity to self-coach and self-direct their own learning.

For teachers new to the profession or new to a position, they are often looking for validation of their practices and for new ideas. Sometimes they don't know what they don't know. Their toolbox usually benefits from new strategies and resources. This situation more often leads to utilizing the coaching skill of *putting ideas on the table.*

That said, we as leaders can be too quick to offer suggestions for new faculty. Just because they are inexperienced does not mean they lack capacity for generating their own ideas. Giving them an opportunity to develop their own solutions can strengthen their skills as problem-solvers and self-directed learners.

Next is a coaching conversation I had with Elisa who was in her third year of teaching.

EXAMPLE 6.1: EXPLORING NEW IDEAS FOR CLASSROOM MANAGEMENT

Observations

Speaker	What was said/done	Rationale for response
Me	"Based on what we have discussed so far, you would like to focus on improving your classroom management to better support all students' voices being heard."	I summarized our previous conversation, identifying a goal and the rationale for the goal.
Elisa	"That's right."	The teacher confirms this account of her goal is accurate.
Me	(paused)	I paused to help formulate a response and give both of us time to think.
Me	"You mentioned that some students tend to blurt out at times, which may lead to others feeling like they cannot share their thinking during instruction."	I *paraphrased* a previous comment.
Elisa	(nods)	

Confirming this information through paraphrasing ensures that the next part of this conversation map—the wondering—is based on agreed-on evidence. Cognitive Coach Ron Lott notes, "You earn the right to pose a question through paraphrasing." Listening deeply through paraphrasing shows the other person that we care about the issue. Through listening, we also develop a solid understanding of the present challenge that has an impact on the quality of the wondering.

Wondering

Speaker	What was said/done	Rationale for response
Me	"Thinking about developing a more equitable experience for all students, how specifically does blurting impact your teaching?"	I started with a more abstract paraphrase (equity), then posed a question to learn more specifically what sources of tension or frustration were present.

Speaker	What was said/done	Rationale for response
Elisa	"Well, it is not good for my blood pressure!"	We both laughed. The teacher's sense of humor indicated she was staying somewhat positive and that she felt comfortable having this conversation with me.
Elisa	"I feel like I cannot get through the curriculum because I am having to redirect these couple of students before I can continue teaching."	
Me	(paused)	I gave us both time to process what was said and formulate a response.
Me	"I am sensing frustration, for both the students because they cannot engage in classroom discussion and for you because you feel like you are not meeting academic expectations." (held up both hands to visualize the dual nature of the challenge)	Because the teacher provided two perceived challenges (lack of equity in student discussion, meeting schoolwide expectations), I used an organizing paraphrase to help frame the thinking.
Elisa	"Correct."	
Me	"Thinking about these two challenges, which one might be the best focus for now? In other words, which challenge, if addressed effectively, would lead to immediate benefits, maybe even for both areas?"	I posed another question, this time to help focus our conversation on one challenge to address at a time.
Elisa	(paused)	I gave time for her to process this proposal.

We discovered through conversation that the teacher was feeling ineffective on multiple levels. From Elisa's perspective, she could not meet her own internal expectations for classroom management, which was leading to lack of progress with external expectations. By posing a question that forced us to choose, she could devote our attention to one challenge and hopefully feel okay about not worrying about the other issue for now.

(Continued)

(Continued)

Speaker	What was said/done	Rationale for response
Elisa	"So, you are suggesting I can pick one area to focus on for improvement, and not worry as much about the other?"	The teacher is clarifying the wondering I posed to her.
Me	"Yes."	
Elisa	"Well, I think if I can improve the blurting then I will feel more successful with the curriculum. We will be able to accomplish more."	The teacher decided what to focus on. She is now in the "driver's seat" and owns the learning process.
Me	"You identified a challenge that seems to influence multiple areas. How does it feel to focus on one thing at a time?"	I acknowledged her capacity for self-directed learning. I also created awareness around the positive feelings she is experiencing.
Elisa	"Yes, I feel like a weight is lifted off my shoulders."	
Me	"Let me know how I might help with the challenge. For example, I'm happy to collect data, such as how many times a student disrupts class as you try a new strategy during a future instructional walk."	I offer an idea for data collection, while acknowledging that she is still in control over how to address the blurting.

There are a couple of things to unpack here.

While I suspected that students blurting during instruction was somewhat of an issue for her, I did not initially understand the additional pressure Elisa had put on herself regarding getting through the curriculum. It seemed to be accelerating her anxiety about classroom management, which led to her feeling even less effective as a teacher. So, by offering Elisa a choice of which issue to focus on, she regained some control over the situation. Conversely, if our discussion had only focused on classroom management, we may never have understood the more important desire of wanting to feel effective.

In a less effective conversation, the leader as a coach might have right away offered three different classroom management strategies to try. But it would not have alleviated the teacher's deeper concern over feeling behind with the curriculum. This is how instructional walks become so important: I have context not just for that teacher's classroom, but for every classroom in the school. I understand some of the dynamics within each space that I would not otherwise have without frequent visits to classrooms and collaborations. For example, knowing about any unhealthy pressures that might be put on Elisa by colleagues about "getting through the curriculum" would have altered my response to the situation, such as being more open to putting ideas on the table for managing these professional relationships.

What is also interesting here is I did not actually provide any ideas for classroom management. That is because that was not the primary challenge. Elisa's goal was *to feel effective*. There are lots of strategies out there for classroom management or improving student discussion. What is often lacking are opportunities for teachers to be supported as they navigate these issues as a professional, to feel like someone who is seen as capable. By offering this chance to figure it out, Elisa came to own and better understand the challenge. She is better set up for success now and in the future.

ACTIVITY 6.2   TEACH TEACHERS HOW TO COACH OTHERS AND THEMSELVES

There are multiple professional learning opportunities to embed coaching skills so that all teachers can start utilizing them with students, families, colleagues, and themselves:

1. Start a meeting with a video of a coaching skill demonstrated from Thinking Collaborative (thinkingcollaborative.com). This website offers excellent short clips, such as on how to notice and respond to body language.

2. Offer to host demonstration lessons and include the lesson plan that describes the intentions for using coaching skills with the students.

3. Provide staff with periodic opportunities for self-assessment around the coaching skills. For example, teachers can rate their own capacity for paraphrasing or posing questions with colleagues during professional learning communities.

It is rewarding when I see teachers implement these coaching skills in their practice. For example, during an instructional walk a teacher was sitting next to a student during a writers' workshop. Everyone was working on how-to books: what they knew a lot about and believed others would value as readers.

I noticed the teacher did a lot of paraphrasing and clarifying of what the student was writing and thinking. She was helping the student find a theme in what he had written, to inform his yet-developed title and final section.

(Continued)

(Continued)

Teacher:	Okay, so one of your sections is about s'mores, something you do when you go camping.
Student:	(nods)
Teacher:	I also see that swimming and setting up the campsite are part of the experience. (She paused.) Thinking about all three of these subtopics, what are you noticing they all have in common?
Student:	(paused to think) They are fun?
Teacher:	They are fun—you are right! Now the question is if you want your entire book to follow that pattern . . ."

While handing my instructional walk to the teacher, I shared my positive observation. "You were teaching the writer first, coaching him and allowing him to construct new thinking."

The teacher (Katelyn Dunham, personal communication, April 14, 2021) replied, "Thanks! Yes, I have been using some of the collaborative norms we have been reviewing this year, like paraphrasing. These norms have been helpful for me to slow down and really listen to my students."

Mid-career teachers—professionals with 5-10 years of experience—are typically more confident in their instruction. They have several resources, strategies, and tools to call on when one approach does not work for at least some of their students. Also, a general observation about mid-career teachers is their transition from trying many ideas for optimal student learning to solidifying their theory of practice. They have found success in some approaches and tend to stick with them.

This has both promise and peril. Promise because, at this stage in their career, they have committed to the profession and believe they make a positive impact on student learning. In addition, teachers with considerable experience have often progressed to a "self-authoring" way of knowing. They have developed a set of beliefs about why they do what they do, holding onto these theories while listening to what colleagues have to share.

The peril is in the potential decrease in their willingness to deviate from what's "tried and true" and consider new approaches. Studies have shown that as people age, they may become more rigid and less mentally flexible when new challenges come up (Kegan & Lahey, 2009).

At the same time, the same studies found that people can maintain flexibility and continue to grow cognitively provided they have the right conditions and support. Critical at this career stage (and really any stage) is *providing data*. People need to see evidence of the impact of their instruction in addition to affirming what's working.

The following coaching conversation with Marcos, a teacher in his 10th year, articulates one example of this type of support.

EXAMPLE 6.2: HOW THE TASK SUPPORTS STUDENT ENGAGEMENT

Observations

Speaker	What was said/done	Rationale for response
Me	"What are you noticing about your practice right now? What's going well, or what's not?"	The initial question is an open invitation to talk about whatever is on his mind at the time.
Marcos	"Well, as you saw the last couple times you visited my classroom, we have deviated from our ELA curriculum resource."	
Me	"Okay." (paused)	I paused to allow the teacher to surface a question or a challenge.
Marcos	"Yeah . . . I think my team would prefer that I stick to the set lessons, but we have enjoyed connecting the reading and the writing."	
Me	"When you say 'we,' you are referring to both the students and you, correct?"	A paraphrase that also clarifies what the teacher is sharing.
Marcos	"Correct. Some of my students have a hard time understanding the relationship between reading and writing, that they are part of a whole."	The teacher reveals the rationale for his decision-making.

(Continued)

(Continued)

Speaker	What was said/done	Rationale for response
Me	(paused) "So, you are feeling some tension with your team as you adapt the curriculum to better meet the needs of your students."	This paraphrase takes Marcos's ideas to a more abstract level.
Marcos	(nods)	

Marcos is conflicted. He wants to be a good team member and a responsive teacher. In his mind, these dual goals may not be compatible. In addition, he may not see his role as a leader on his team, as a contributor to his colleague's knowledge about literacy instruction. The following wondering helps Marcos expand his perspective, from teacher to potential leader.

Wondering

Speaker	What was said/done	Rationale for response
Me	"As a responsive teacher your priority is the students. What evidence are you finding that is supporting these efforts?"	I started by affirming Marcos's identity. The question posed offers a pathway for identifying data that supports his decision-making.
Marcos	(pauses) "That's a good question."	Time is provided to allow Marcos to call up positive results he observed during instruction.
Marcos	"Well, I am finding that we are getting through more of the curriculum because we are combining reading and writing. For example, we had extra days for independent learning projects because our informational text unit was done."	A quantitative data point—more time—serves as possible evidence of a more efficient and effective student learning experience.
Me	"And you believe that students learned just as much as in previous years with this literacy unit of study?"	I followed up with another question, this time to ensure that his results were valid.
Marcos	"Actually, better with some students. We had so many more conversations as a class about reading like a writer and writing for a reader. It was fun. I think that enjoyment and the connections increased students' engagement, which showed in their final writing project."	The follow-up question elicited even more data points to support his professional decision-making.

Through the wondering around data, Marcos discovered that he had several artifacts that supported his decision-making: more instructional time, improvement in students' writing, improved classroom discussion, and an internal sense of joy. The presenting information offered a next step for us: how we might organize this information that both validated his work and could serve as an opportunity to present these findings to his team.

Next Step

Speaker	What was said/done	Rationale for response
Me	"You have found several data points that support your work, including more time to teach, your students' writing, your classroom discussions, and the joy felt by you during instruction."	I used an organizing paraphrase to help structure our thinking.
Marcos	"That's right."	
Me	"Thinking about your teammates, how might they respond if you presented this information to them?"	I posed another question, to connect his learning with the potential to influence how his colleagues might view this work.
Marcos	"Well, that's what we are supposed to be doing during PLCs [professional learning communities], right?"	Marcos refers to the schoolwide focus on professional collaboration, likely to support his own willingness to bring new ideas to the team.
Me	"That's how I understand it."	
Marcos	"I think it could go a number of ways: they might be put off that I am presenting positive results after deviating from the curriculum resource. (pauses) They might also acknowledge the results and ask more about what we did."	Marcos is anticipating obstacles and opportunities as he decides whether to share his work.
Me	"Both of these responses seem possible. Of the two, which do you think is more likely?"	I continue to organize our thinking, both for clarity and to ensure there are always choices within these coaching conversations.

(Continued)

(Continued)

Speaker	What was said/done	Rationale for response
Marcos	(pauses) "We really have a good team. Likely, they will be at least interested if not excited about the results and want to know more."	In addition to Marcos's new openness to sharing his work, he visibly relaxed when visualizing his teammates' positive response: he sat back, and his shoulders dropped.
Me	"I would agree with your assessment of your team. Just in case you experience the other possibility, is that something you can live with?"	I pose one more question here. Experience has told me that follow-through does not always occur without a decent amount of planning for possible pushback.
Marcos	(pauses) "I think so. The data is pretty persuasive, and we have to start having these conversations at some point, about teaching the student vs. the resource."	In this statement, Marcos recognizes his own role as a leader within his team. He also knows that these issues will keep coming up until they are addressed.

In some schools, the expectation is on the "official" school leader to ensure that professional teams are operating as expected. The reality is that a principal or other administrator only has so much influence on the interactions that occur among faculty.

That is why when leading like a coach, we strive to find every opportunity to support our teachers as leaders. They are the ultimate decision makers in the classroom. We can support them by first "inquiring into the problem," including seeing more perspectives beyond our own, and then exploring alternative theories to the problem that "begins to build the trust needed to tackle it together" (Robinson, 2018, p. 43).

In Marcos's situation, we did not fully understand the issue until we unpacked it. Genuine curiosity and commitment to supporting his capacity set him up to become the authority figure. I sometimes think of myself as an editor of a publishing company, and the teacher or staff member as the author. (The root word of authority is "author.") We cannot write the book for them; they must craft their own narrative for sustainable change to take hold.

And every educator is somewhere along their own journey of continuous improvement. Opportunities for supporting even our most veteran faculty can lead to growth that we might not have anticipated without an effective approach to communicating feedback. This leads into the next and final example for this chapter: balancing idea sharing with respect for the many years of experience some of our teachers bring to the classroom.

ACTIVITY 6.3 — ASK TEACHER TEAMS TO SHARE WINS WITH COLLEAGUES

Team wins—and any form of being recognized for an accomplishment—is powerful. We see it all the time in the sports world: the legacies of professional teams, the historic undefeated season, the 80-year championship drought finally redeemed with a championship ring.

A similar experience can be facilitated with our teacher teams. Asking them to share their wins as well as the process that led them to success can have an impact on the rest of the school. A big benefit is that a team will likely have (a) evidence to support their success and (b) a pathway (process) that describes the work that went into reaching their goals.

These narratives can serve as celebrations for staff meetings. For example, one team described how they struggled with engagement with a few of their students (lack of commitment to their learning, misbehaviors, etc.). Then they introduced self-directed independent projects in their classrooms. Students now had voice and choice in what to learn about. Every day, time was built into the schedule for projects.

As a leader, you can guide teams with questions to help articulate their story and their win.

- How did you come across this innovative idea?
- What challenge were you trying to address?
- Previously, what had you tried and why do you think it did not work?
- How did you know that this new approach was successful?
- What suggestions would you give to your colleagues if they are thinking about trying this innovation in their classrooms?

EXAMPLE 6.3: A BETTER WAY TO ASSESS

A classroom teacher, Marianne, asked me if she should try digital portfolios for her students' writing or stay with print only. "Which option do you think is best?" We were meeting for our fall individual conference, the first of three for the year.

I was impressed that this teacher, with decades of experience, wanted to pursue an innovative assessment approach. Just the fact that she helps her students curate portfolios, documenting their work throughout the school year and taking time to reflect on their growth periodically, was admirable. To go digital with their writing had many additional benefits, such as a wider audience and more ways of capturing student thinking.

Marianne was exploring improvement not just through her own sense of the world but also through imagining her students' experiences. She understood that if students are not clear about what quality looks like in their learning, they may always be dependent on someone else to tell them. Approaching portfolio assessment means letting go of at least some control of the classroom so students become primary decision makers. These are brave decisions that need to be handled with care.

With Marianne's question, it initially felt like an open invitation to consult. Being perceived as someone with credibility and authority is an ego booster. Who doesn't like feeling like an expert? It is also a tricky situation. We as the coach/leader can come into the situation with too much enthusiasm and not enough understanding for what the teacher really needs. We might also deprive them of the opportunity to solve the challenge themselves. At the same time, we have ideas to share. Why withhold information that might prove fruitful?

This balancing act when working with our veteran faculty (and all teachers) can be supported by *paying attention to self and others*. That means being mindful of our own goals, feelings, and emotions as well as all the physical/nonverbal signs our colleagues present when we are working with them. For example, if they fold their arms while speaking, are they subtly communicating that they are "closed off" from any further feedback? The content and preceding conversation would help determine that. In this final example, we see how awareness of ourselves, the other person, and the environment support better conversations, again through the three primary coaching skills of paraphrasing, pausing, and posing questions. (The dialogue begins after the teacher asked me about portfolios.)

Observations

Speaker	What was said/done	Rationale for response
Me	"You are looking for the best environment for your students to post their work and reflect."	I paraphrased here to show the teacher I was listening and to confirm their thinking.
Marianne	(nodded)	
Me	"I am wondering about the pros and the cons of each option— digital or print portfolios." (paused)	I paraphrased my own thinking within an objective lens to hopefully decrease any stress.
Marianne	"With writing portfolios, the students will probably reflect more. They just seem to enjoy reading over their own writing in print vs. the computer. But it is difficult for me to assess their work in this way. With digital, it is the opposite: I can see how they are doing, but I am concerned they won't self-assess as well."	Based on this evidence, it seemed the paraphrase fostered deeper thinking around the instructional options.
Me	(paused)	There was a lot of information here, so I paused to allow the teacher to process what she just shared and for me to consider my next response.

As stated previously, we as coaches and leaders are not without our own ideas. We can take positions on these types of issues.

At this point in the conversation about portfolio assessment with the teacher, I sensed that we needed that additional option to consider. The teacher seemed genuinely interested in what I might have to contribute to the conversation. Still, I wanted to be sure that my input was welcome.

(Continued)

(Continued)

Wondering

Speaker	What was said/done	Rationale for response
Me	"You want your students to reflect on their writing, and you also want to be able to access their thinking and work through digital means."	I organized the teacher's thinking—two goals—through a *paraphrase*.
Marianne	(nodded)	The teacher confirmed nonverbally, supported with a pause.
Me	"Would you be okay with me sharing one possibility with you?"	I posed a question to ask for permission to share an idea and positioned the idea as "one possibility" to ensure the teacher still felt empowered.
Marianne	"Sure, that's fine."	
Me	"What I know about portfolio assessment and writing is that it is an opportunity for authentic reflection. It can be helpful if in print because it is private; our inhibitions go down. We know we are not going to be judged, and subsequently we feel safe to share whatever is on our mind. "Knowing this, is there a way to allow students to organize their writing in a binder, while expecting them to select one piece periodically and share it online, say once every six weeks? That way you both can assess it and they have control in their writing lives."	
Marianne	She paused, her eyebrows raised. "Oh, I didn't consider that." Here, I noticed she did not jump at the idea. She crossed her arms and her shoulders closed in a bit.	From her body language I suspected she was not ready to accept this idea wholeheartedly. We ended our time together on a positive note but without resolution about the issue.

WISDOM FROM THE FIELD: THE COACH IN THE OPERATING ROOM

Dr. Atul Gawande discovered that he had arrived at his professional peak as a surgeon. He wanted to continue to improve, so he asked a former trusted teacher to observe him in the operating room. After surgery both doctors discussed what went well and what could be improved. Even though Dr. Gawande's coach had rarely done the surgery himself, "that one twenty-minute discussion gave me more to consider and work on than I'd had in the past five years" (Gawande, 2011).

How can you enter a coaching conversation with both confidence and humility? Related, how might you become more coachable—who in your world could serve in this capacity for you? Jot down some ideas and thoughts in your journal.

EXAMPLE 6.3 (CONTINUED)

Next Step

Was I too quick to offer an idea? Maybe. Her nonverbal cues, such as her closed posture, showed someone who might have become less open to this option. Still, she had asked the question. I clarified what she was asking, and I did ask permission to offer an idea.

Before our winter conference, I read through my observational notes from my frequent informal visits to her classroom. This information, along with her initial goal of developing relationships, guided me to scale back my question as I checked back on our previous conversation.

Speaker	What was said/done	Rationale for response
Me	"So what did you decide regarding portfolios?"	I followed up on our previous conversation.
Marianne	"I decided to focus on organizing the writing online and to keep it simple. I will provide some scaffolding for this assessment process, such as modeling how to write a reflective statement under the document camera."	

(Continued)

(Continued)

Speaker	What was said/done	Rationale for response
Me	"Kids will definitely appreciate your modeling and guidance. That alone can improve the quality of their writing."	I affirmed her decision and listed reasons why it could work.

What matters here is the teacher felt empowered to decide. Whether she went with digital portfolios only or a combination of print and online, Marianne believed that the approach she selected would work.

Beliefs are powerful. They guide our everyday decision-making. Every teacher in our school believes they are doing what is best for their students. Yet there may be a better teaching strategy available than the one currently in use. How do we go about communicating this? Suggesting one approach over the teacher's current approach may change what happens in the classroom, but it is less likely to change a teacher's belief system. Similar versions of the same practice will keep popping up. Like the game whack-a-mole, we try to hit one over the head while the next one pops up. The belief system of the teacher is not changing—it is "underneath the surface."

In this example, both approaches in my estimation were fine. In fact, going only digital may prove to be the better choice with an authentic audience plus the efficiencies of organizing writing online. Another next step might be to help the teacher set up some type of mini-action research cycle if they are interested. For example, she could assess the students' writing in the fall, winter, and spring, and then compare these results to the previous year's results. Communicating feedback is a continuous cycle of inquiry, not a one-and-done experience.

SPECIAL NOTE: WHEN A TEACHER IS NOT IMPROVING

While most of your teachers will continue to grow with support, there may be one or more faculty members who do not.

Education is a challenging profession. Not everyone is a great fit for the classroom. If you have established trust with the teacher, created clarity around a priority, affirmed their efforts toward promising practices, communicated feedback in ways they can hear it, and they still are not meeting even minimal expectations for effective instruction, then it may be time to develop a plan for improvement (or whatever process your district recommends for this situation).

This would be the only time in which you are not using instructional walks to support teaching and learning. We have transitioned from engaging in professional improvement to ensuring minimal expectations are being met. If over time the teacher has been successful with the plan for improvement, you can then discuss moving back to a more coach-like approach to classroom visits that includes instructional walks.

Work closely with your human resources director or superintendent during this entire process. You want your leader's full support if the teacher is unable to show adequate improvement in their performance, especially if it leads to a recommendation for nonrenewal of the teacher.

CONCLUSION: TRUST THE PROCESS

Providing someone with feedback is not a simple transfer of information. Are they ready to accept it? How do we know? If they have requested feedback, are they *really* ready to consider it, meaning they have questioned their current theory of action and are interested in a new instructional process?

All we can do is trust the process, both the coaching tools we employ and the professionals with whom we engage. I sometimes fall into thinking that a cycle of inquiry or conversation must end in a clear resolution. But I need to play the long game. Keep showing up, develop and sustain relationships, and have faith that improvement will happen. We can only find out if teachers are ready to take risks by taking similar risks ourselves.

SUCCESS INDICATORS FOR COMMUNICATING FEEDBACK

- Documentation is organized and serves the conversation, not the other way around. Changes in practice may not happen immediately while communicating feedback, especially with more experienced teachers. That is why it is important to meet periodically with faculty to talk about their work. Fall, winter, and spring conferences can be fruitful opportunities for dialogue. I find it helpful to keep track of what teachers are sharing regarding their goals and their plan within the instructional walk notes I capture digitally. Then you

(Continued)

(Continued)

can ask at the next meeting, "How is what you are doing now making a difference?" The teacher is then communicating what has changed versus you telling them what you think is occurring.

- When meeting with teachers, they will sometimes display "a-ha" moments. Eyes widen, mouths agape, eyebrows up when what you are both talking about shifts their thinking. This is not unlike the "lightbulb moments" when teaching students. It will more likely occur not because you resolved a problem for them but because they solved the challenge themselves. The most successful coaching experiences uncover new perspectives versus offering new ideas.

- As your own capacity for communicating feedback improves, you might find others asking you to work with others or even themselves. For example, a faculty member whose student-teacher is struggling with instruction might ask you to "coach them up," as they are not feeling effective and need a new perspective. This could be for the student-teacher or for them—coaches need coaches, too.

 # Reflective Questions

Consider the following questions to promote reflection. You can respond to them in writing and/or in conversation with colleagues.

1. What are three key takeaways for you after reading this chapter?

2. Prepare wonderings for two teachers after reflecting on their practice or reviewing their instructional walks. How might each question help that teacher become more self-directed?

3. After a coaching conversation with one of your teachers, take postmeeting notes that describe your visual observations and emotional cues of this faculty member. Based on these notes, how well-received was the feedback you communicated?

HELP TEACHERS BECOME LEADERS AND LEARNERS

Central to my conception of a good school and a healthy workplace is community. In particular, I would want to return to work in a school that could be described as a community of learners, a place where students and adults alike are engaged as active learners in matters of special importance to them and where everyone is thereby encouraging everyone else's learning. And I would readily work in a school that could be described as a community of leaders, where students, teachers, parents, and administrators share the opportunities and responsibilities for making decisions that affect all the occupants of the schoolhouse.

—Barth (1990, p. 9)

It was my last year at my previous school. We had received the individual test scores from the recent state exam. The results determined not only our rating on our state report card but also whether we would be eligible for Title I recognitions and grant dollars made possible through federal initiatives such as Race to the Top.

I learned from a previous supervisor that you can roughly determine how you did as a school by going through each student's results. You place them in one of four groups—advanced, proficient, basic, or minimal—based on their literacy and math scores. You obviously wanted many of your students in the advanced or proficient group, but you also wanted to see your students with various challenges stay out of minimal or basic. As I leafed through each report, I wrote down the scores in one of four categories. Nearing the end of the reports it became clear that we would not be achieving preferred outcomes. A few students had no scores reported for one test. We must have missed a make-up!

Sitting there rifling through test results, I was putting a lot of responsibility on myself. *Should I have expected more practice sessions with the teachers?* Yet I knew test prep was not particularly effective and did not lead to long-lasting learning.

> These test scores are largely out of our control. At best, we can use them to understand broad trends and patterns about our curriculum and maybe glean insights about different groups of students to determine what inequities we might need to address.

These test scores are largely out of our control. At best, we can use them to understand broad trends and patterns about our curriculum and maybe glean insights about different groups of students to determine what inequities we might need to address.

What is within our control? The results that we see every day in our schools. Teachers can and do describe the impact of their instruction: "Her eyes lit up when she finally understood the concept." "He is able to read more accurately, something I noticed during independent reading." And yet these results are typically neither communicated nor appreciated by those outside of education. Subsequently, we are stuck with the external measures, these tools that paint a broad and vague picture of the complex schools we lead.

Or are we? What if we could develop the capacity of teachers to take back some control over their outcomes from the classroom? Through a coaching stance, how might we support colleagues to lead their own learning and become leaders in the school?

A JOURNEY TO EXCELLENCE

Teaching with urgency does not mean rushing through lessons; it does mean being mindful that how and what we are teaching in every instructional moment

*is worthwhile for our students. We're not in a race
to the top; we're on a journey to excellence.*

—Routman (2014, p. 29)

We have two examples of teachers on a "journey to excellence." Both Jason (Chapter 3) and Mary Beth (Chapter 5) became more intentional in their instruction to better meet their students' needs. They slowed down their practice to examine it and make changes. The support they received helped them become students of their own practice, to a point where they could begin to coach themselves. Table 7.1 conveys their journeys to professional excellence and becoming leaders and learners.

If we can scale individual teacher improvement like this to a collective capacity for continuous learning, the results would be better than any test score or teacher evaluation. A school or even a district could take back their narrative instead of feeling like they had no control over the outcomes. No more running the "testing treadmill," chasing scores

Table 7.1 How two teachers became instructional leaders and self-directed learners

The C.O.A.C.H. process	Jason	Mary Beth
Create Confidence Through Trust	The instructional leadership team offered teachers choice in instructional strategies to try.	Action research was optional; teachers had autonomy in selecting a research question.
Organize Around a Priority	Graphic organizers were selected as tools to help Jason's students monitor their thinking when reading and organize their writing ideas.	Shared writing of personal narratives was a practice adopted in response to students' apathy around reading and writing.
Affirm Promising Practices	The small successes that were recognized in the beginning led to improvements in instruction (i.e., location of the organizers).	Students responded to Mary Beth's vulnerability in her personal writing by being open and honest in their own struggles.
Communicate Feedback	Jason continued his own learning by requesting to observe colleagues employing similar practices.	Students made gains and were able to exit out of this reading intervention class.
Help Teachers Become Leaders and Learners	Jason's public vulnerability positioned him as an instructional leader in the eyes of his colleagues.	Mary Beth has since written multiple times for educational journals about her teaching experience.

> *No more running the "testing treadmill," chasing scores and staying in one place. Instead, you could have a community of professionals who owned their results because they had the authority and expertise to change how their story is told.*

and staying in one place. Instead, you could have a community of professionals who owned their results because they had the authority and expertise to change how their story is told.

This is really the only way to schoolwide success—together. It is also a scary proposition. We are releasing some of the responsibility for the results of our efforts. Yet it also makes sense. Who is in the classroom? Not us as leaders. If the goal is self-directedness in our students, the best way we can model this is by entrusting our teachers with the same level of responsibility.

If this sounds too much "u-rah-rah" or unattainable, I can understand. I was skeptical myself, until I saw it myself as well as learned about it from other educational leaders. Letting go, as unnerving as it is, is also cathartic. Teachers and students will surprise you. You might even be able to leave the test reports in their binders or online and be able to relax more outside of school, knowing you and your teacher leaders are in this together.

The rest of this chapter presents two examples that describe collective journeys toward more effective and enjoyable learning experiences for everyone involved. Teacher self-assessment and a residency model to professional development are highlighted within the context of a real school and district, respectively. While they each have a distinct approach, the common thread is a collective capacity for continuous renewal, where professionals lead and learn together. They also happen to serve as examples of initiatives incorporating the five principles of this book: (1) create confidence through trust, (2) organize around a priority, (3) affirm promising practices, (4) communicate feedback, and (5) help teachers become leaders and learners.

EXAMPLE 7.1: TEACHER SELF-ASSESSMENT (WILMOT ELEMENTARY SCHOOL, JEFFERSON COUNTY PUBLIC SCHOOLS, DENVER, COLORADO)

Matt Cormier was the principal at Wilmot Elementary School, part of a large district of 80,000 students. He engaged in regular leadership coaching with Sam Bennett. During one of their conversations, they agreed that the current teacher evaluation system was not enough to support professional growth. They needed something more.

That something else was a renewal of their educator evaluation system. Instead of one or two formal and unannounced classroom observations, Matt would visit five to six times a year that were less formal and more aligned with the teacher's goals instead of only a rubric. Instead of the required conferences at the beginning of the year to check off the boxes for a student learning objective and a professional practice goal, they would begin with a letter of reflection that shared why they got into education in the first place: delving into their deepest beliefs about teaching and learning before engaging in a conversation around their practices. These shifts resembled a more authentic and meaningful approach to teacher supervision and support.

Create Confidence Through Trust

Matt started this process with an opt-in approach the first year. "I wanted it to feel safe and not stressful." A few teachers participated initially. With a successful pilot, the following year was an opt-out approach to the process. "Everyone participated; no one opted out."

One of the biggest concerns around the new process was, of all things, writing the context letter. Teachers cited the time needed to write it, which Matt acknowledged by committing to a set date next time that included breakfast and coffee. Maybe just as important, Matt wrote his own context letter. This was a demonstration of vulnerability, which all the teachers got to read. It reflected Matt's own challenges and successes in this profession. He also communicated his philosophy verbally at staff meetings. "Why not learn from failure and trying?" he recalls sharing with teachers. All these actions removed some of the obstacles and increased confidence in this approach.

Organize Around a Priority

While the new process shifted more of the authority to teachers to assess their own practice, it was still grounded in the language of their evaluation tool.

In the beginning of the school year, teachers referenced the district-approved educator evaluation rubric as they completed their self-assessment of their own performance. Matt read their assessment, checked for alignment with his own ratings of that teacher, and then submitted both into the system if there was mutual agreement. At the

(Continued)

(Continued)

same time, he submitted the formal observation requirement. "That's it," he noted. "I am done with my formal evaluations for the year, with the exception of the spring assessment which largely resembles the fall."

Matt also pointed out that he would not use this approach with a teacher he has concerns about. "I only used this process with effective and known educators." In fact, he did not even consider this process until he had five years' experience as a principal in Wilmot Elementary. The time he had devoted to visiting classrooms and talking with teachers about their practice not only established trust but also created clarity about their school goal and focus.

To prepare for classroom visits, Matt asked his teachers: "What do you want me to look for in the classroom?" The teachers would again reference the educator evaluation tool when describing their priority around their professional learning goal. Because of the general nature of these rubrics, they can be aligned with just about any school-specific goal. Indicators of success are further articulated in the tool and between Matt and his teachers.

Affirm Promising Practices

Because the stance to the new approach to teacher supervision relied on self-assessment, everyone needed to be clear on what the promising practices looked like in the classroom. Any disagreement about proficient versus advanced within student engagement, for example, was clarified when both Matt and his teachers discussed the ratings from the fall discussion.

Still, there needed to be a way to affirm the teachers' current practices with both their beliefs and what was outlined within the observational framework for instruction. In addition, there was the matter of staying current with what educational research was finding to be effective in the classroom.

So Matt and his teachers planned for multiple observational visits that first considered each educator's context letter documenting their beliefs, the practices they agreed would best support what learning goal they were striving to achieve, and the research to support this work. Matt's written observations after a classroom visit were followed up by a reflection letter that summarized his thinking and posed questions around:

● The alignment between their beliefs in the context letter and their practices observed

- The alignment between the practices observed and the instructional framework
- The alignment between beliefs, practices, and research available in the literature

These reflection letters served somewhat like a longer version of an instructional walk. They were not a "gotcha" because the teacher was directing the destination and the pathway for this supervision process. The major portion of the evaluation process took place in the fall with the self-assessment. "The teachers and I already know where they are at as professionals: proficient or advanced," Matt notes. "We have moved past that and now are engaged in a conversation about practice." These affirmations were not a pat on the back; they validated what was observed in relation to agreed-on standards to get a more accurate understanding of the instructional reality in the classroom.

Communicate Feedback

When a promising practice was not present in the classroom, there was a clear process for inquiring into the "why" of the teacher's decision-making. Matt and the faculty moved from compliance with a set list of professional expectations to engagement in the thinking of each educator. Egos were reduced. Curiosity was the primary mindset so that a coaching conversation might follow.

For example, one teacher in Matt's school was not posting learning targets. "If I had come in on my designated day to observe this teacher, do you think there would have been learning targets posted on the board? You bet." Matt realized that because trust had increased and authority rested more with the teacher, the need to look good had taken a back seat to each teacher being more honest about their practice. "I can now go into that teacher's classroom and simply ask them, 'Why are you not putting up learning targets?' It is no longer about following directions but about understanding their beliefs as to why they do or do not do something." Because of the openness of the professional climate, both teachers and Matt were more candid about their thinking and knew where each person was coming from.

The research came in when Matt explained his position. He appreciated the summaries from The Marshall Memo (marshallmemo.com), as well as the book guides developed at The Main Idea (themainidea.net). As a busy principal, Matt needed to be able to quickly access the latest literature and studies to support his position on an issue that needed

(Continued)

(Continued)

more clarity. These conversations happened either in writing (after Matt's reflection letter) or in person, both post-observation.

In one conversation, I asked Matt if he would ever go back to the more traditional approach to teacher supervision and evaluation. "No way," Matt quickly responded. "I go back to what my coach, Sam Bennett, asked me at the beginning of this work: 'Do you think your current process is getting you the results you are looking for?' They were not, so I won't."

Help Teachers Become Leaders and Learners

Matt's success with the new evaluation system encouraged him to keep learning about the process. For example, he invited his superintendent to join him during classroom observations. The purpose was for the district administrator to coach him in his capacity to effectively support teaching and learning. Matt also recognized that this is ongoing work. His role as a formal leader carried with it the perception of positional power, which can inhibit candid professional interactions. As Matt reflected from where he started, "The system I had was about compliance. It didn't feel good when I hear teachers say to me that they're nervous. When I walked in, I noticed a change either in the voice or just in some of the moves. If I've got a computer with me, there's a change."

Being aware of this dynamic helped ensure Matt's focus was on building and fostering trust within the school. This work led to teachers becoming more confident and self-directed in making instructional decisions they believed best met their students' needs.

ACTIVITY 7.1 — ALIGNING CURRICULUM RESOURCES WITH BELIEFS AND PRACTICES

In the spring, teachers are asked to develop budgets for the following school year. They request dollar amounts and specific resources based on what they believe will positively affect student learning.

But are their requests aligned with your shared beliefs as a school, or the promising practices you have found effective? My experience tells me this mindset takes time to develop and can benefit from continued guidance.

One approach to improving this process is to expect teachers to show alignment between what they would like to purchase and these beliefs and practices. It can be an internal process for not only ensuring school funds are used well but also to reflect on why they are doing what they are doing.

Here is an example. What is your assessment on this alignment?

Belief/practice	Resource requested
A child's written story can be used to teach phonics and skills.	Workbooks for phonics instruction and phonemic awareness (3 × $495 = $1,485)

At first glance, this request does not appear aligned with the belief or practice, which calls for an authentic approach to phonics instruction. But we do not have to say "no." In the spirit of developing self-directedness, we can ask our faculty to reflect on their requests. In this situation, I might ask, "How does this resource align with this shared belief or any other?" It is now incumbent on the teacher or team to make their case. If they cannot, you have the moral authority to deny it. If teachers are persistent, encourage them to craft a belief that (a) aligns with this resource and (b) everyone can agree on.

This process would seem most appropriate for major resource requests only. Smaller purchases and implementation can be discussed during the instructional walk process.

WISDOM FROM THE FIELD: LETTING GO AS LEADERSHIP

During the 2020 Tokyo Summer Olympics (which took place from July 23 to August 8, 2021), gymnast Simone Biles withdrew from the team competition. She felt she couldn't perform her best after a bad landing on a vault. "I knew that the girls would do an absolutely great job, and I didn't want to risk the team a medal because of my screwups," Biles said. "Because they've worked way too hard for that." Biles knew she would receive criticism for her decision, yet she prioritized the team over others' expectations of her (Aten, 2021).

How can we let go of some attention and authority in our roles to create space for others to lead? Are we confident enough to be humble? Jot down some ideas and thoughts in your journal.

EXAMPLE 7.2: RESIDENCY MODEL FOR PROFESSIONAL DEVELOPMENT (RIVER EAST TRANSCONA SCHOOL DIVISION IN WINNIPEG, MANITOBA, CANADA)

As much as we want to support personalized teacher learning, there is an understandable desire to balance autonomy with the need for all classrooms to provide an equitable student learning experience. This means facilitating district-wide professional development that every educator participates in and implements with consistency and regularity.

That does not mean professional learning must be delivered exclusively from an external source. In the River East Transcona School Division in Winnipeg, Manitoba, Canada, teachers and administrators have spent a decade building a province-wide literacy culture. Under the leadership of individuals such as Jason Drysdale (personal communication, December 24, 2019), assistant superintendent; Allyson Matczuk (personal communication, December 27, 2019), literacy interventionist; and many others, efforts were made to focus on improving the capacity of all educators to work more effectively with readers and writers.

To assist in this process, they brought in Regie Routman and colleagues to lead weeklong residences in hub schools. Satellite schools also engaged in this work, joining fellow Winnipeg faculty during the residencies in which Routman and colleagues demonstrated effective lessons and coached principals on how to conduct instructional walks. These buildings agreed to a three-year commitment to implementing authentic and balanced literacy instruction. (You can learn more about this specific literacy residency model in Routman's (2014) book *Read, Write, Lead: Breakthrough Strategies for Schoolwide Literacy Success*.)

Create Confidence Through Trust

With the support of the superintendent, assistant superintendent Jason Drysdale could be an engaged member of the process. For example, Jason participated in the initial professional learning sessions facilitated by Routman and colleagues. That also included sitting in classrooms for demonstration lessons and talking with the observers about what just happened. In addition, he communicated his expectations for everyone to participate. For example, the building principals were expected to be present for the sessions and commit to the work. "People clearly got the message that this work is not going away. There was some pretty strong messaging there," Jason recalled. He also wrote about these experiences and shared his understandings with all schools.

Commitment and trust were more easily attained because they grounded the work in the success out of Reading Recovery. This literacy intervention embodied many of the principles they wanted to implement in every classroom: students engaged with authentic texts, addressing all aspects of literacy, efficient use of instructional time, and robust professional development that included peer observation. Also worth noting is that Reading Recovery has received high marks from the educational research community for its effectiveness across many environments. Multiple sources of evidence supporting this district-wide initiative accelerated trust.

Organize Around a Priority

Using in-district literacy data, professional development leader Allyson Matczuk learned that while students progressed as readers once out of Reading Recovery, their writing plateaued. This information was shared with Jason and other district leaders, which became the impetus for developing a priority around improving writing instruction and adopting a residency model.

This approach required clarity if it were to be a true priority in Winnipeg. Routman's (2014) explanation of this process (p. 273) created a shared understanding among all schools involved.

- Examine current beliefs and practices and achievement data schoolwide.
- View exemplary reading and writing practices in diverse classrooms and schools.
- Continue to talk about what has been seen and heard in host classrooms and apply learning to their classrooms and school.
- Read and discuss professional articles that provide the research, theory, and practices that support and expand the work.
- Try out practices with support of colleagues and coaches.
- Gain an understanding of what literacy practices look like at every grade level.
- See student progress over time.

These characteristics of the residency model served as steps within the improvement plan. There were no surprises. At the same time, teachers had flexibility and choice within this structure. Teachers could choose

(Continued)

(Continued)

to be part of a demonstration lesson or to observe one, for example. Student progress, measured with interim writing assessments, validated their work and provided information on what specifically to work on next.

Affirm Promising Practices

"Principals are the lynchpin," declared Allyson when we spoke about the Winnipeg experience. "And if they are going to support this process, they need to know what to look for, which means building knowledge about the instructional practices and strategies we are all learning about." Jason concurred. "We needed to build principal capacity and ensure that leaders engaged in this substantive, ongoing work."

Jason and other district leaders committed money and other resources to support the time necessary to implement this work effectively. For instance, they coordinated coverage so principals could build a habit of visiting classrooms. The residency leaders joined them, coaching each leader in the instructional walk process. In addition, accountability from Jason came in the form of "homework," in which every school leader was expected to bring back one example of an instructional walk to a district administrative meeting. Together they discussed their experience: what was working, what wasn't, and how they might improve the process for next time. As expertise was developed among the administrators' group, certain principals were asked to serve as peer leaders for their colleagues.

One of the peer leaders is Mario Beauchamp (personal communication, December 13, 2019). A K-5 principal, Mario schedules his instructional walks for the following week on Friday. "Timing was somewhat of an issue for me in the beginning," he acknowledged. Striking a balance with the need for routine, he regularly reminds himself to celebrate teachers' and students' attempts as well as their successes. "I want to encourage risk-taking, that mistakes can be a good thing." Mario keeps his comments during classroom visits authentic and positive by reading aloud all his observations to the class. "It is like I have written a love letter to the whole class. As I read my notes aloud, the kids and staff beam with pride." Classrooms will sometimes post Mario's notes on a bulletin board. He believes that his visits with professional learning communities are more positive and productive because he is affirming the promising practices he finds during instruction.

Communicate Feedback

Another peer leader at Winnipeg was Arlis Folkerts (personal communication, December 2, 2019). She had the opportunity to learn about and implement instructional walks as an assistant principal under the mentorship of Margaret Fair, her principal at John de Graff Elementary School. When Arlis was appointed principal at Radisson School, the school became the Early Years "hub school," with a strong focus on implementing Routman's fundamentals for reading and writing instruction and learning. Routinely visitors from other divisions would visit the school to see the profound impact this work can have for improving student engagement and success.

Like Mario, she differentiated her approach with instructional walks, especially in how she communicated her observations. "It's like descriptive feedback for kids, but for teachers, so I wanted to vary how this information was delivered. I would use sticky notes, public praise without writing anything down, or full written narratives, all with the purpose of highlighting teachers' innovative practices." For example, co-teaching was implemented around the same time as the schoolwide literacy initiative, in which a special education teacher teams up with the general classroom teacher to deliver instruction for all students, including students with disabilities. Arlis could tailor her comments to acknowledge their collaborative work.

This ability to differentiate feedback based on what people needed is what makes instructional walks so powerful, notes Arlis. "Instructional walks helped us focus collectively on instruction, teacher *and* student. They also helped me form positive relationships with students and staff. It didn't overwhelm teachers. In addition, we learned to appreciate that every year was a new group of kids, and that we couldn't teach them the same way as previous years." While Allyson, Jason, Mario, and Arlis acknowledged that instructional walks are only one piece of the puzzle, it was critical for ensuring clarity of common language for the ongoing work and for sustaining these efforts over time.

Help Teachers Become Leaders and Learners

What was the impact of their efforts? Allyson analyzed student learning results and educators' actions within these hub and satellite schools. She then compared them with the other buildings that did not engage in this work at the same depth (described as "self-directed schools"). Her findings revealed two of the following conclusions:

- Students in the hub and satellite schools made greater gains in their writing, grades K-3, than self-directed schools over a three-year period.
- The principal's involvement as educational leader was critical to enduring teacher change and ongoing student improvement.

(Continued)

(Continued)

Additional results were observed by Routman (2014) during her several years of working with the Winnipeg area school divisions (p. 276), such as the following:

- More students leaving kindergarten as writers and readers
- Teachers identifying students first as readers and writers and not by labels or family background
- Increased writing for an authentic audience and purpose, partially evident in the amount of published writing in hallways
- Greater alignment of beliefs and practices at and across grade levels and use of common language with understanding

The influence of this project spread across the division. For instance, Jason shared that the middle schools in their division were interested in the work the elementary schools were doing, based on the students' writing performance as they matriculated into the secondary level. Seeing these results over time deepened teachers' confidence in their work, which further reinforced the impact of their decision-making. It became an appreciative cycle of continuous learning.

SPECIAL NOTE: THE IMPORTANCE OF THE SUPERINTENDENT

Just as it is critical for teachers to have the support of their principal, it is crucial for the district superintendent to be a champion for a leader and their school. Being a champion does not mean taking a laissez-faire stance regarding a leader's efforts. It involves advocating for a school's collective efforts that are aligned with a district's mission and vision and what is known to be effective for student learning.

Equally important for the superintendent is to be a buffer from negative factors. For example, larger districts will sometimes move ineffective teachers into schools where strong instructional leadership is present. The hope is that a school with a strong track record will hold that teacher accountable for improvement. Sometimes referred to as "the passing of the lemons," this is disruptive to a school community that has worked hard to build a cohesive culture. When this happened in a school that had worked with Routman (2014), she and the new principal met with the superintendent and requested that he "protect the school" by not placing inept teachers there in the future (p. 278). A superintendent has an obligation to ensure each leader has their support and does not make decisions that derail their efforts.

RETHINK THE TYPICAL SCHOOL IMPROVEMENT PLAN

The typical school improvement plan sometimes treats goals and outcomes as foregone conclusions instead of professional inquiry. For example, they often contain a S.M.A.R.T. goal: Specific, Measurable, Attainable, Relevant, and Time-Bound.

Logically, these plans make sense. "If I do 'A,' then 'B' will be the result." Yet there are potential problems with this approach to school improvement.

1. Too often the measures utilize assessments that are not sensitive enough or closely aligned with our actions that we take as a school. For example, if we use a screener assessment to determine the amount of growth from fall to spring in overall reading proficiency, will that tool reflect our efforts to improve fluency? Maybe, maybe not.

2. If we want our goal to be attainable, there is a chance that we will set the bar too low. Attainable connotes minimal, a standard benchmark. Wouldn't we rather strive for something aspirational, a noble outcome to achieve? Maybe what needs to be attainable are the anticipated steps to take to achieve a goal.

One suggestion for rethinking your school improvement plan is to "W.O.O.P." it. Developed by Dr. Gabrielle Oettingen, a professor of psychology, W.O.O.P. stands for wish, outcome, obstacles, plan. The key difference in this approach to improvement, in my experience, is *obstacles*. As you and your leadership team are thinking about how to achieve some level of growth as a school—your wish and an outcome that relates to the wish—what might stand in your way? Anticipating possible challenges after describing a vision and goal (referred to as "mental contrasting") can help leaders prepare a plan that will more likely succeed.

For example, during the pandemic, my school's wish was to ensure a safe and equitable learning experience regardless of where we were teaching and learning from. One of our obstacles we listed was, "What if we have to go all virtual for an extended period of time?" To plan for this contingency, we developed two schedules at each grade level: one for in-person instruction and one for virtual. And wouldn't you know it, we did have to teach virtually for six weeks at one point. (For more information about W.O.O.P., see Oettingen's (2014) book *Rethinking Positive Thinking: Inside the New Science of Motivation*.)

Our school improvement plans need to be adaptive for the complexity of our work. Whether you use W.O.O.P. or another approach, it is helpful to embed flexibility and a capacity for anticipating potential challenges as part of your plan.

CONCLUSION: A TRUER CALLING

A leader's goal is for their teachers to be able to lead themselves and become a collective, sustainable group of continuous learners. I have heard other leaders go as far as to describe this goal as "working myself out of a job."

I question this direction. I am not trying to work myself out of a job as much as uncovering what my real job is. It is a constant process of reflecting on experience and then acting on these insights to discover my truer calling as a leader.

What I have discovered is what you have here: a rethinking of our roles, of what I believe right now to be our real work in schools. I hope what I have shared provides you with a pathway for your own journey to excellence.

SUCCESS INDICATORS FOR HELPING TEACHERS BECOME LEADERS AND LEARNERS

- Teachers will become empowered when releasing responsibility for how a school operates. For example, they may become more engaged with district-level decisions, sharing their ideas on relevant issues. Teachers feeling empowered . . . this is a good thing. To help them frame their positions, consider setting up regular times to listen to faculty and offer suggestions.

- Dissatisfaction with the status quo may lead to teachers wanting to explore better resources and practices for all classrooms, not just theirs. As an example, they might start to see the reading curriculum as building-wide versus at one grade level or department. We can support this initiative by providing time and resources for multiple grade levels or departments to meet and discuss their work.

- Related, school visits may become a more common request. These might be within district if it is a larger one, or in a neighboring city. Describe these visits as opportunities to learn for everyone.

 # Final Reflective Questions

Consider these final questions to promote reflection about what you have learned from this book. You can respond to them in writing and/or in conversation with colleagues.

1. What three major insights did you gain after reading this book?

2. Considering these insights, what two actions do you plan to make as a result? What is your timeline for taking action? (Try to be specific. For example, "I will engage in one instructional walk for every teacher in my building by the end of the month.")

3. If you were to recommend this book to one colleague, who would it be? How might they be a sounding board and thought partner in both of your efforts to lead more like a coach?

CONCLUSION

What Will Be Your Legacy?

In my first year in my current school, a well-known retired teacher, Don Hawkins, passed away. He had taught agriculture at the high school. Don was involved in building community awareness around important environmental issues and putting them into action.

Specifically, two oak savannas were established on district property; one was situated on my school grounds. Oak savannas are the natural habitats that once existed without disruption in our area of Wisconsin and across other parts of the region. Burr oaks, purple coneflower, prairie grasses, and other natural plants populate the rolling landscape. Paths have been forged through the savanna for students and other visitors. Whitetail deer are spotted every year.

At the front of the entrance to the main pathway to the savanna is a kiosk. Pictures of the flora and fauna people might find in the savanna are displayed with their common and scientific names. At the top of the kiosk is "Don Hawkins Oak Savanna" in large letters.

If you ask someone what Don Hawkins's legacy is, what might they say? His name on top of the kiosk? The savanna itself, one of the first features I noticed when I initially visited Mineral Point for an interview?

I would argue that it is none of the above, at least by themselves. This teacher's legacy is the people who have committed to the calling of learning about oak savannas and preserving this space. Students, volunteers, and their current teacher from the agriculture department come down at least once a year to collect the seeds from the flowers. These seeds are started the next season, and the plants are sold as a fund-raiser. District staff continue to maintain the grounds, keeping the path cleared of weeds and adding new features to the space.

Anyone's true legacy is the influence they had on how others operate in their community and maybe even the world. This influence comes from investing in people first, believing in their potential for positive change for themselves and for others. I know the benefits because I am a direct beneficiary: the visible pride that comes with a sense of independence and interdependence. This is what learning and leading is about: teaching others and, through that process, teaching ourselves.

REFERENCES

Allen, J. (2016). *Becoming a literacy leader: Supporting learning and change.* Stenhouse.

Allington, R. L., & Gabriel, R. E. (2012). Every child, every day. *Educational Leadership, 69*(6), 10-15.

Aten, J. (2021, July 27). Simone Biles's surprising Olympic withdrawal is an extraordinary example of effective leadership. *Inc.* https://www.inc.com/jason-aten/simone-biles-tokyo-olympics-leadership.html

Baeder, J. (2018). *Now we're talking! 21 days to high-performance instructional leadership.* SolutionTree.

Barth, R. S. (1990). *Improving schools from within: Teachers, parents, and principals can make the difference.* Jossey-Bass.

Bennett, S., & Tovani, C. (2020). *Behind the scenes of why do I have to read this?* Stenhouse Teacher's Corner Podcast. https://stenhouse.libsyn.com/website/behind-the-scenes-of-why-do-i-have-to-read-this

Bernhardt, V. (2015). Toward systemwide change. *Educational Leadership, 73*(3), 56-61.

Binford, W. (Ed.). (2021). *Hear my voice/Escucha mi voz: The testimonies of children detained at the southern border of the United States.* Workman.

Brown, B. (2017). *Braving the wilderness: The quest for true belonging and the courage to stand alone.* Random House.

Bryk, A., & Schneider, B. (2002). *Trust in schools: A core resource for improvement.* Russell Sage Foundation.

Burn, C. (Ed.). (2019). *The moth presents occasional magic: True stories about defying the impossible* (Vol. 1). Crown Archetype.

City, E. A., Elmore, R. F., Fiarman, S. E., & Teitel, L. (2009). *Instructional rounds in education: A network approach to improving teaching and learning.* Harvard Education Press.

Cohen, J., & Goldhaber, D. (2016). Building a more complete understanding of teacher evaluation using classroom observations. *Educational Researcher, 45*(6), 378-387. https://doi.org/10.3102/0013189X16659442

Cohen, J., Hutt, E., Berlin, R., & Wiseman, E. (2020). The change we cannot see: Instructional quality and classroom observation in the era of common core. *Educational Policy.* Advance online publication. https://doi.org/10.1177/0895904820951114

Collins, B. (Ed.). (2003). *Poetry 180: A Turning Back to Poetry.* Random House Trade.

Costa, A. L., Garmston, R. J., Hayes, C., & Ellison, J. (2016). *Cognitive coaching: Developing self-directed leaders and learners.* Rowman & Littlefield.

Danielson, C. (2016). Charlotte Danielson on rethinking teacher evaluation. *Education Week, 35*(28), 20-24.

De la Peña, M. (2015). *Last stop on market street*. Penguin.

Del Prete, T. (2013). *Teacher rounds: A guide to collaborative learning in and from practice*. Corwin.

DeWitt, P. (2020). *Instructional leadership: Creating practice out of theory*. Corwin.

Drago-Severson, E., & Blum-DeStefano, J. (2016). *Tell me so I can hear you: A developmental approach to feedback for educators*. Harvard Education Press.

DuFour, R., Dufour, R., Eaker, R., Many, T., & Mattos, M. (2016). *Learning by doing: A handbook for professional learning communities at work* (3rd ed.). Solution Tree.

Duhigg, C. (2012). *The power of habit: Why we do what we do in life and business*. Random House.

Duhigg, C. (2016, February 25). What google learned from its quest to build the perfect team. *The New York Times Magazine*. https://www.nytimes.com/2016/02/28/magazine/what-google-learned-from-its-quest-to-build-the-perfect-team.html

Fogg, B. J. (2020). *Tiny habits: The small changes that change everything*. Mariner Books.

Gabriel, R. E., & Woulfin, S. L. (2017). *Making teacher evaluation work: A guide for literacy teachers and leaders*. Heinemann.

Garrett, C. (2021). Relevant curriculum is equitable curriculum. *Educational Leadership, 78*(6), 48-53.

Gawande, A. (2011, September 26). Personal best: Top athletes and singers have coaches. Should you? *The New Yorker*. https://www.newyorker.com/magazine/2011/10/03/personal-best

Grissom, J. A., Egalite, A. J., & Lindsay, C. A. (2021). *How principals affect students and schools: A systematic synthesis of two decades of research*. The Wallace Foundation. https://www.wallacefoundation.org/knowledge-center/Documents/How-Principals-Affect-Students-and-Schools.pdf

Grissom, J. A., & Loeb, S. (2017). Assessing principals' assessments: Subjective evaluations of teacher effectiveness in low- and high-stakes environments. *Education Finance and Policy, 12*(3), 369-395. https://doi.org/10.1162/EDFP_a_00210

Hall, T. (2019). *Writing to persuade: How to bring people over to your side*. Liveright.

Hall, W. (2012). When it comes to change, are you a committed sardine? [Blog post]. *ALLTHINGSPLC*. https://www.allthingsplc.info/blog/view/179/when-it-comes-to-change-are-you-a-committed-sardine

Hallinger, P., Hosseingholizadeh, R., Hashemi, N., & Kouhsari, M. (2018). Do beliefs make a difference? Exploring how principal self-efficacy and instructional leadership impact teacher efficacy and commitment in Iran. *Educational Management Administration & Leadership, 46*(5), 800-819. https://doi.org/10.1177/1741143217700283

Hattie, J. (2021). *Visible learning meta^x*. Corwin. https://www.visiblelearn
ingmetax.com/Influences

Hiebert, J., & Stigler, J. W. (2017). Teaching versus teachers as a lever
for change: Comparing a Japanese and a U.S. perspective on improving instruction. *Educational Researcher, 46*(4), 169-176. https://doi
.org/10.3102/0013189X17711899

Hill, H., & Grossman, P. (2013). Learning from teacher observations:
Challenges and opportunities posed by new teacher evaluation systems.
Harvard Educational Review, 83(2), 371-384. https://doi.org/10.17763/
haer.83.2.d11511403715u376

Ibarra, H., & Scoular, A. (2019). The leader as coach: How to unleash innovation, energy and commitment. *Harvard Business Review, 97*(6), 110-119.
https://hbr.org/2019/11/the-leader-as-coach

Johnston, P., Champeau, K., Hartwig, A., Helmer, S., Komar, M., Krueger, T.,
& McCarthy, L. (2020). *Engaging literate minds: Developing children's
social, emotional, and intellectual lives, K-3*. Stenhouse.

Katz, J. (2011). *Meet the dogs of Bedlam Farm*. Henry Holt.

Kegan, R., & Lahey, L. L. (2009). *Immunity to change: How to overcome it
and unlock the potential in yourself and your organization*. Harvard
Business Review Press.

Khachatryan, E. (2015). Feedback on teaching from observations of teaching:
What do administrators say and what do teachers think about it? *NASSP
Bulletin, 99*(2), 164-188. https://doi.org/10.1177/0192636515583716

Kim, A., & Gonzales-Black, A. (2018). *The new school rules: 6 vital practices
for thriving and responsive schools*. Corwin.

Knight, J. (2010). *Unmistakable impact: A partnership approach for dramati-
cally improving instruction*. Corwin.

Krebs, D., & Zvi, G. (2020). *The genius hour guidebook: Fostering passion,
wonder, and inquiry in the classroom* (2nd ed.). Eye On Education.

Lipton, L., & Wellman, B. (2007). How to talk so teachers listen. *Educational
Leadership, 65*(1), 30-34.

Ma, X., & Marion, R. (2021). Exploring how instructional leadership affects teacher efficacy: A multilevel analysis. *Educational
Management Administration & Leadership, 49*(1), 188-207. https://doi
.org/10.1177/1741143219888742

Marshall, K. (2013). *Rethinking teacher supervision and evaluation: How
to work smart, build collaboration, and close the achievement gap*.
Jossey-Bass.

Marzano, R. J., Pickering, D., & Pollock, J. E. (2001). *Classroom instruction
that works: research-based strategies for increasing student achievement*. ASCD.

Merriam-Webster. (n.d.-a). Affirm. In *Merriam-Webster.com dictionary*.
Retrieved September 20, 2021, from https://www.merriam-webster.com/
dictionary/affirm

Merriam-Webster. (n.d.-b). Priority. In *Merriam-Webster.com dictionary*.
Retrieved August 13, 2021, from https://www.merriam-webster.com/
dictionary/priority

Oettingen, G. (2014). *Rethinking positive thinking: Inside the new science of motivation*. Penguin Random House.

Perkins, D., & Reese, J. (2014). When change has legs. *Educational Leadership, 71*(8), 42-47. https://www.ascd.org/el/articles/when-change-has-legs

Qadach, M., Schechter, C., & Da'as, R. (2020). Instructional leadership and teachers' intent to leave: The mediating role of collective teacher efficacy and shared vision. *Educational Management Administration & Leadership, 48*(4), 617-634. https://doi.org/10.1177/1741143219836683

Robinson, V. (2018). *Reduce change to increase improvement*. Corwin.

Robinson, V. M. J., Lloyd, C. A., & Rowe, K. J. (2008). The impact of leadership on student outcomes: An analysis of the differential effects of leadership types. *Educational Administration Quarterly, 44*(5), 635-674. https://doi.org/10.1177/0013161X08321509

Routman, R. (2012, June 25-26). *Keynotes and workshop sessions*. Literacy and Leadership Institute Conference, Madison, WI. www.cesa6.org/regie

Routman, R. (2014). *Read, write, lead: Breakthrough strategies for schoolwide literacy success*. ASCD.

Stevens, K. B., & Tracy, M. (2020). *Still left behind: How America's schools keep failing our children*. American Enterprise Institute. https://www.aei.org/research-products/report/still-left-behind/

Stronge, J. (2019, September 30). *Teacher & principal evaluation: What works?* [Webinar]. https://www.cesa6.org/

Sweeney, D. (2010). *Student-centered coaching: A guide for K-8 coaches and principals*. Corwin.

Tschannen-Moran, M. (2014). *Trust matters: Leadership for successful schools*. Jossey-Bass.

U.S. Department of Education. (2019). *NAEP report card: 2019 NAEP reading assessment*. Institute of Education Sciences, National Center for Education Statistics. https://www.nationsreportcard.gov/reading/nation/scores/

Van Allsburg, C. (1991). *The wretched stone*. Houghton Mifflin Harcourt.

Vecsey, G. (2010, June 4). Wooden as a teacher: The first lesson was shoelaces. *The New York Times*. https://www.nytimes.com/2010/06/05/sports/ncaabasketball/05wizard.html

Vodicka, D. (2006). The four elements of trust. *Principal Leadership, 7*(3), 27-30.

Walker, R. (2020, August 3). The late John Thompson was larger than life, as plenty of people in Louisiana can attest. *The New Orleans Advocate*. https://www.nola.com/sports/article_bac48a26-ebd9-11ea-ad94-574c5f35aeb7.html

Whitaker, T. (2012, February). *Speaking session, Wisconsin school administrators elementary principals' conference*, Elkhart Lake, WI.

Wiest, B. (2018, April 23). 8 traits that are scientifically proven to predict future success. *Forbes*. https://www.forbes.com/sites/briannawiest/2018/04/23/8-traits-that-are-scientifically-proven-to-predict-future-success/?sh=3563a0d7655a

Yi, H., Mo, D., Wang, H., Gao, Q., Shi, Y., Wu, P., Abbey, C., & Rozelle, S. (2019). Do resources matter? Effects of an in-class library project on student independent reading habits in primary schools in Rural China. *Reading Research Quarterly, 54*(3), 383–411. https://doi .org/10.1002/rrq.238

Zinsser, W. (1998). *Inventing the truth: The art and craft of memoir.* Mariner Books.

INDEX

A SAGE Publishing Company

Helping educators make the greatest impact

CORWIN HAS ONE MISSION: to enhance education through intentional professional learning.

We build long-term relationships with our authors, educators, clients, and associations who partner with us to develop and continuously improve the best evidence-based practices that establish and support lifelong learning.

Leadership That Makes an Impact

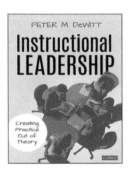

PETER M. DeWITT

This step-by-step how-to guide presents the six driving forces of instructional leadership within a multistage model for implementation, delivering lasting improvement through small collaborative changes.

JOHN HATTIE & RAYMOND L. SMITH

Based on the most current Visible Learning® research with contributions from education thought leaders around the world, this book includes practical ideas for leaders to implement high-impact strategies to strengthen entire school cultures and advocate for all students.

DOUGLAS FISHER, NANCY FREY, DOMINIQUE SMITH, & JOHN HATTIE

This essential hands-on resource offers guidance on leading school and school systems from a distance and delivering on the promise of equitable, quality learning experiences for students.

STEVEN M. CONSTANTINO

Explore the how-to's of establishing family empowerment through building trust, and reflect on implicit bias, equitable learning outcomes, and the role family engagement plays.

MICHAEL FULLAN, JOANNE QUINN, & JOANNE MCEACHEN

The comprehensive strategy of deep learning incorporates practical tools and processes to engage educational stakeholders in new partnerships, mobilize whole-system change, and transform learning for all students.

JOANNE QUINN, JOANNE MCEACHEN, MICHAEL FULLAN, MAG GARDNER, & MAX DRUMMY

Dive into deep learning with this hands-on guide to creating learning experiences that give purpose, unleash student potential, and transform not only learning, but life itself.

DAVIS CAMPBELL & MICHAEL FULLAN

The model outlined in this book develops a systems approach to governing local schools collaboratively to become exemplars of highly effective decision making, leadership, and action.

DAVIS CAMPBELL, MICHAEL FULLAN, BABS KAVANAUGH, & ELEANOR ADAM

As a supplement to the best-selling *The Governance Core*, this guide will help trustees and superintendents adopt a governance mindset and cohesive partnership.

To order your copies, visit **corwin.com/leadership**

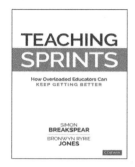

SIMON BREAKSPEAR & BRONWYN RYRIE JONES

Realistic in demand and innovative in approach, this practical and powerful improvement process is designed to help all teachers get going, and keep going, with incremental professional improvement in schools.

JAMES BAILEY & RANDY WEINER

The thought-provoking daily reflections in this guided journal are designed to strengthen the social and emotional skills of leaders and create a strong social-emotional environment for leaders, teachers, and students.

MARK WHITE & DWIGHT L. CARTER

Through understanding the past and envisioning the future, the authors use practical exercises and real-life examples to draw the blueprint for adapting schools to the age of hyper-change.

ALLAN G. OSBORNE, JR. & CHARLES J. RUSSO

With its user-friendly format, this resource will help educators understand the law so they can focus on providing exemplary education to students.

MICHAEL FULLAN & MARY JEAN GALLAGHER

With the goal of transforming the culture of learning to develop greater equity, excellence, and student well-being, this book will help you liberate the system and maintain focus.

TOM VANDER ARK & EMILY LIEBTAG

Diverse case studies and a framework based on timely issues help educators focus students' talents and interests on developing an entrepreneurial mindset and leadership skills.

THOMAS HATCH

By highlighting what works and demonstrating what can be accomplished if we redefine conventional schools, we can have more efficient, more effective, and more equitable schools and create powerful opportunities to support all aspects of students' development.

LYN SHARRATT

Explore 14 essential parameters to guide system and school leaders toward building powerful collaborative learning cultures.

CORWIN